RECORDED VERSIONS GUITAR ®

AUTHENTIC TRANSCRIPTIONS
WITH NOTES AND TABLATURE

SELECTIONS FROM

indigo girls ®

1200 curfews

Music transcriptions by **Dave Whitehill**, **Fred Anderson**, and **Joe Deloro**

Cover photo by **Lance Mercer**

ISBN 0-7935-6638-X

HAL•LEONARD®
CORPORATION

7777 W. BLUEMOUND RD. P.O. BOX 13819 MILWAUKEE, WI 53213

Visit Hal Leonard Online at
www.halleonard.com

INDIGO GIRLS 6:30

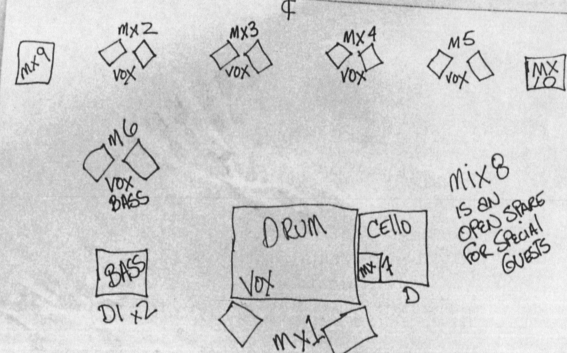

¢

MX9 MX2
VOX MX3
VOX MX4
VOX M5
VOX MX10

M6
VOX
BASS

BASS
DI x2

DRUM
VOX

CELLO
MX 7
D

MIX 8
IS AN
OPEN SPARE
FOR SPECIAL
GUESTS

MX1

indigo girls® 1200 curfews

CONTENTS

9	Closer to Fine
14	Galileo
24	Ghost
36	I Don't Wanna Know
42	Joking
47	Jonas and Ezekial
57	Least Complicated
68	Mystery
77	Power of Two
83	Pushing the Needle Too Far
89	Strange Fire
96	This Train Revised
109	Virginia Woolf
120	World Falls
125	GUITAR NOTATION LEGEND

Photo Lance Mercer

Photo Lance Mercer

Photo Susan Alsner

Photo Lance Mercer

Amy, Emily & Michelle Malone
Photo Susan Alsner

Gail Ann Dorsey   Photo Susan Alzner

Jimmy "Jam" Descant
Photo Susan Alzner

Photo Lance Mercer

Photo Lance Mercer

Sara Lee
Photo Lance Mercer

Photo Lance Mercer

Geoff Trump   Photo Susan Alsner

Photo Susan Alsner

Photo Lance Mercer

Amy & Russell Carter
Photo Susan Alsner

Photo Lance Mercer

Photo Susan Alsner

Emily & Amy   Photo Susan Alsner

Amy and Gerard McHugh
Photo Lance Mercer

Photo Susan Alsner

Jane Scarpantoni
Photo Lance Mercer

Photo Lance Mercer

Emily
Photo Susan Alsner

Photo Lance Mercer

Emily, Amy, Jane Scarpantoni
Photo Lance Mercer

Emily & Amy   Photo Susan Alsner

**Suzanna Santos - Warm Springs, Shelly
Means - Snoqualmie, Winona LaDuke - Honor
the Earth, Margaret Flint Knife Saluskin of
Lyle Point, Chris Peters - 7th Generation Fund**
Photo Lance Mercer

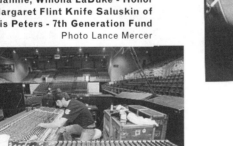

Niles Wood   Photo Susan Alsner

Photo Lance Mercer

Jerry Marotta
Photo Susan Alsner

Photo Susan Alsner

Photo Lance Mercer

Jerry Marotta   **Jane Scarpantoni**   **Amy**   **Emily**   **Sara Lee**

Photo Lance Mercer

Closer to Fine

Words and Music by Emily Saliers

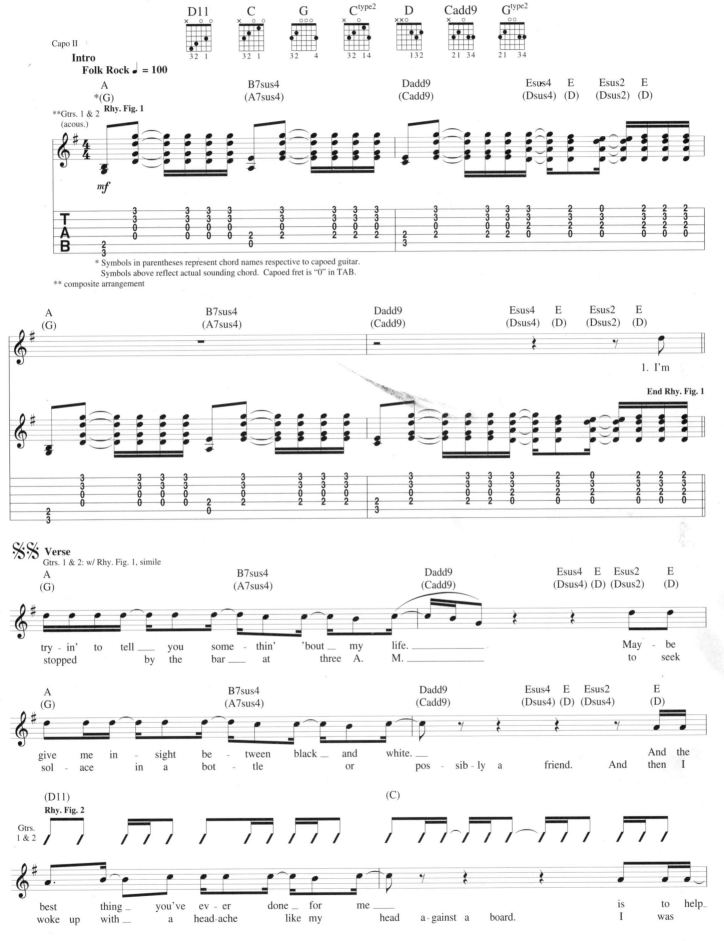

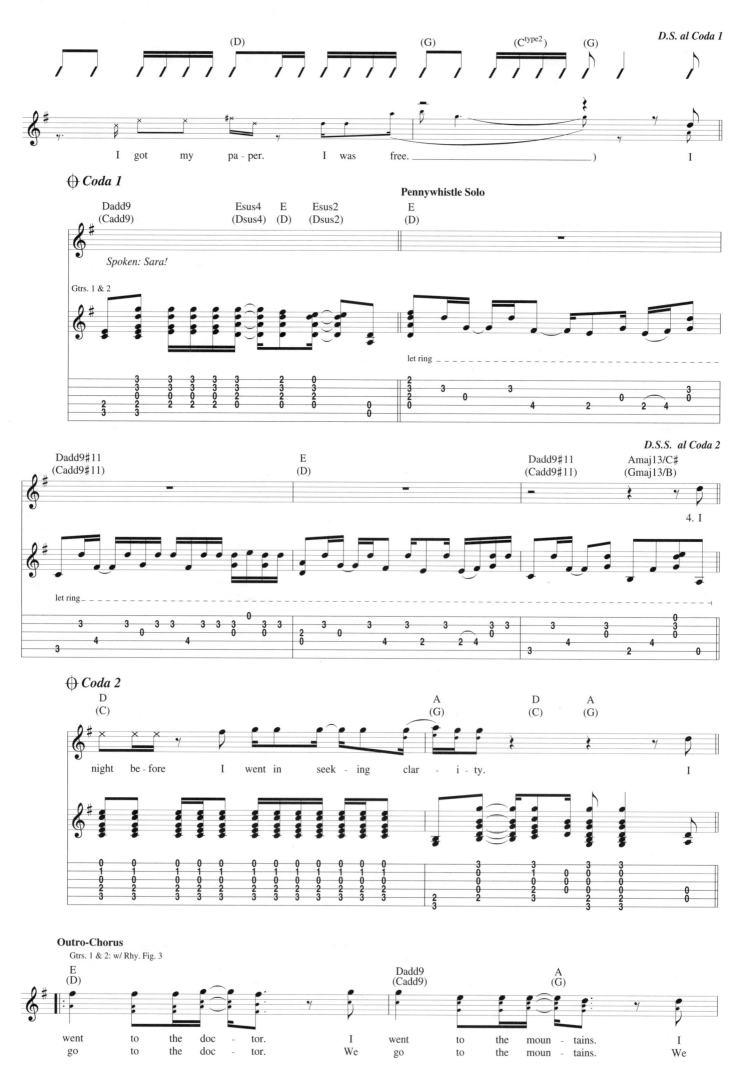

Galileo

Words and Music by Emily Saliers

* Symbols in parenthesis represent chord names respective to capoed guitar (Gtr. 1).
Symbols above reflect actual sounding chord. Capoed fret is "0" in TAB.

** Chord symbols in double parentheses represent chord names respective to Gtr. 2.

vi - sion, king of in - sight. ___ Yeah!

Verse

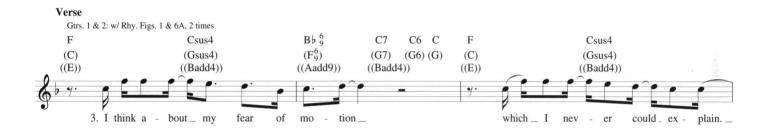

3. I think a - bout ___ my fear of mo - tion ___ which ___ I nev - er could ___ ex - plain.

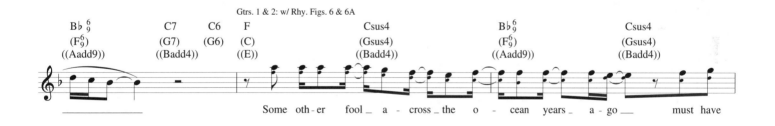

Some oth - er fool ___ a - cross ___ the o - cean years ___ a - go ___ must have

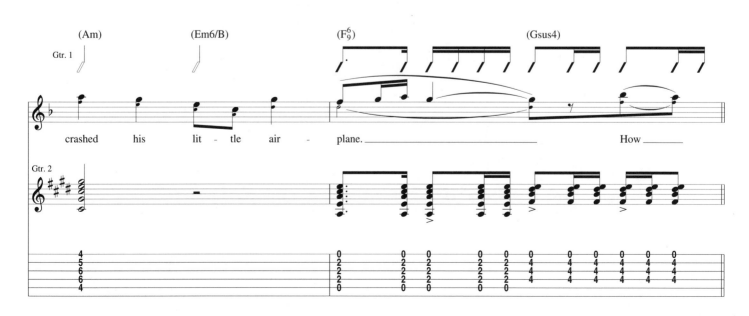

crashed his lit - tle air - plane. ___ How ___

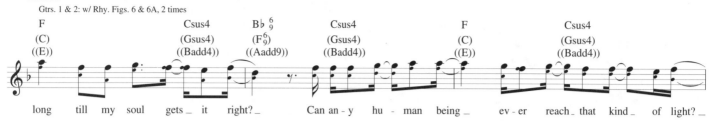

long till my soul gets _ it right? _ Can an - y hu - man being _ ev - er reach _ that kind _ of light? _

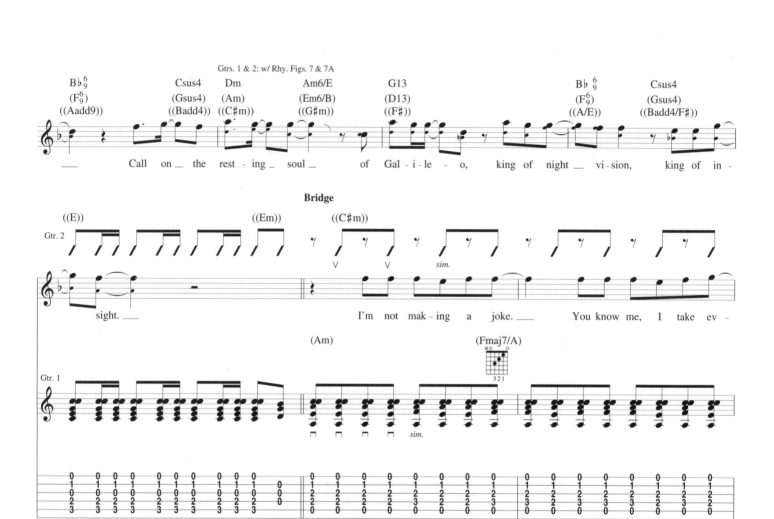

_ Call on _ the rest - ing _ soul _ of Gal - i - le - o, king of night _ vi - sion, king of in -

Bridge

sight. _ I'm not mak - ing a joke. _ You know me, I take ev -

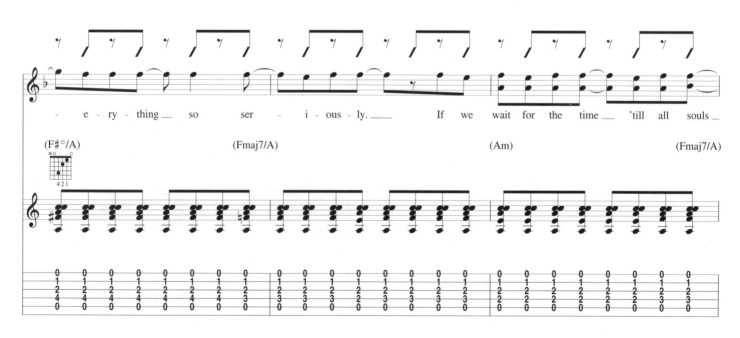

- e - ry - thing _ so ser - i - ous - ly. _ If we wait for the time _ 'till all souls _

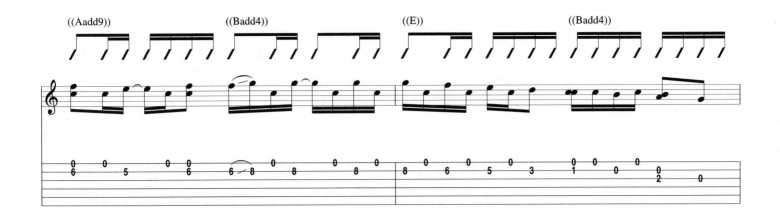

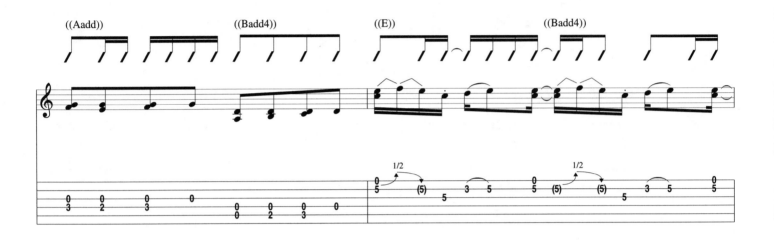

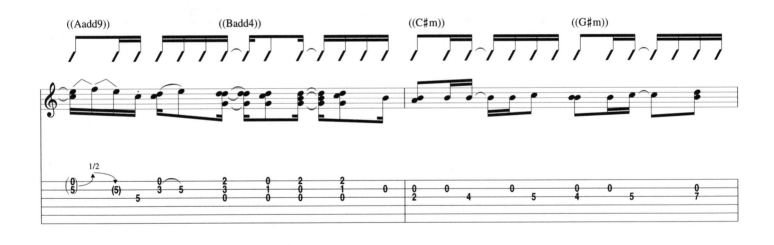

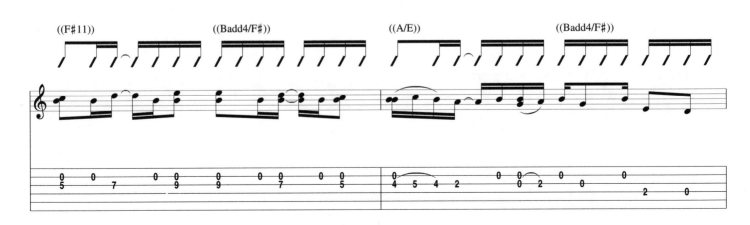

Outro-Chorus

Gtrs. 1 & 2: w/ Rhy. Figs. 6 & 6A, 2 times

F   Csus4   Bb 6/9   Csus4   F   Csus4
(C)   (Gsus4)   (F 6/9)   (Gsus4)   (C)   (Gsus4)
((E))   ((Badd4))   ((Aadd9))   ((Badd4))   ((E))   ((Badd4))

long 'till my soul gets _ it right? _ An-y hu-man being _ ev-er reach _ the high-est light? _

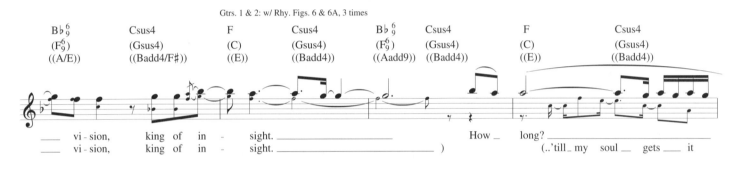

Gtrs. 1 & 2: w/ Rhy. Figs. 7 & 7A

Bb 6/9   Csus4   Dm   Am6/E   G13
(F 6/9)   (Gsus4)   (Am)   (Em6/B)   (D13)
((Aadd9))   ((Badd4))   ((C#m))   ((G#m))   ((F#11))

_ 'Cept for _ the Gal-i-le - o, _ God rest his _ soul, king of night _
(rest-ing soul _ of Gal-i-le - o King of night _

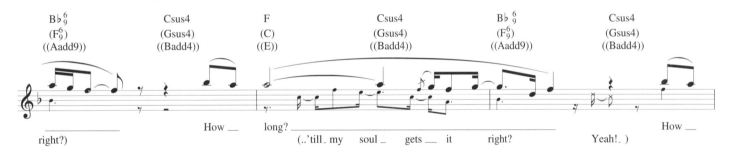

Gtrs. 1 & 2: w/ Rhy. Figs. 6 & 6A, 3 times

Bb 6/9   Csus4   F   Csus4   Bb 6/9   Csus4   F   Csus4
(F 6/9)   (Gsus4)   (C)   (Gsus4)   (F 6/9)   (Gsus4)   (C)   (Gsus4)
((A/E))   ((Badd4/F#))   ((E))   ((Badd4))   ((Aadd9))   ((Badd4))   ((E))   ((Badd4))

_ vi - sion, king of in - sight. _ How _ long? _
_ vi - sion, king of in - sight. _) (..'till _ my soul _ gets _ it

Bb 6/9   Csus4   F   Csus4   Bb 6/9   Csus4
(F 6/9)   (Gsus4)   (C)   (Gsus4)   (F 6/9)   (Gsus4)
((Aadd9))   ((Badd4))   ((E))   ((Badd4))   ((Aadd9))   ((Badd4))

_ How _ long? _ How _
right?) (..'till _ my soul _ gets _ it right? Yeah! _)

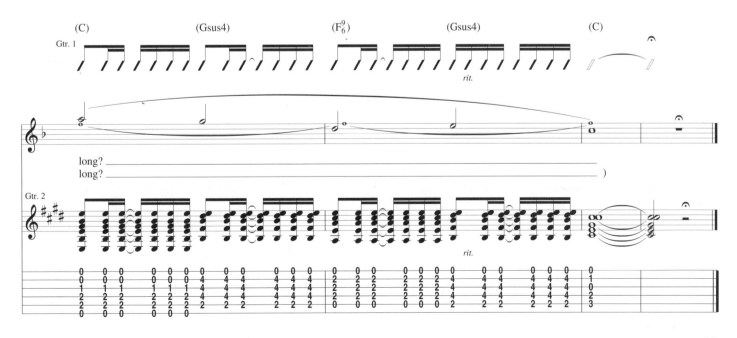

(C)   (Gsus4)   (F 9/6)   (Gsus4)   (C)

Gtr. 1

rit.

long? _
long? _)

Gtr. 2

rit.

Ghost

Words and Music by Emily Saliers

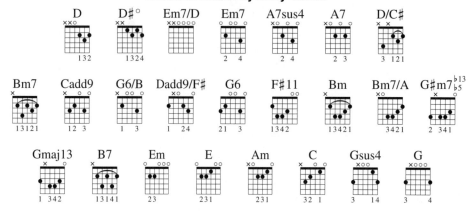

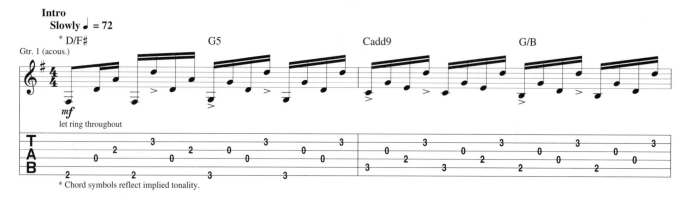

* Chord symbols reflect implied tonality.

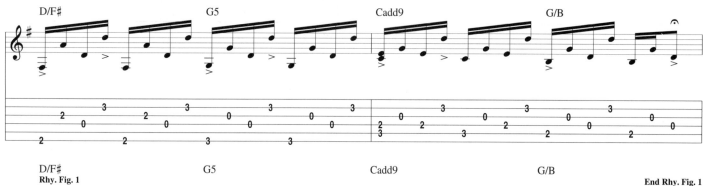

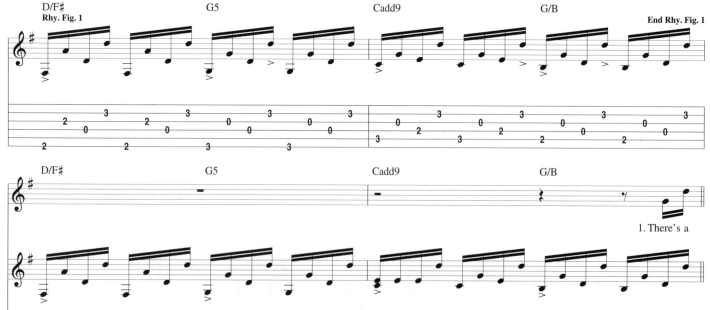

1. There's a

Verse

Gtr. 1: w/ Rhy. Fig. 1, 3 times, simile

let - ter on ___ the desk ___ top I dug out of ___ a drawer; ___ the last truce.

___ we ev - er came ___ to from our ad - o - les - cent war. ___ And I start ___

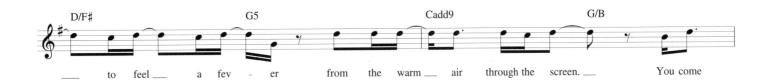

___ to feel ___ a fev - er from the warm ___ air through the screen. ___ You come

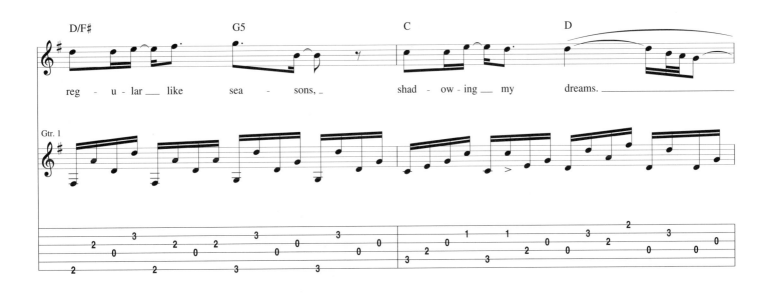

reg - u - lar ___ like sea - sons, ___ shad - ow - ing ___ my dreams. _____

Gtr. 1

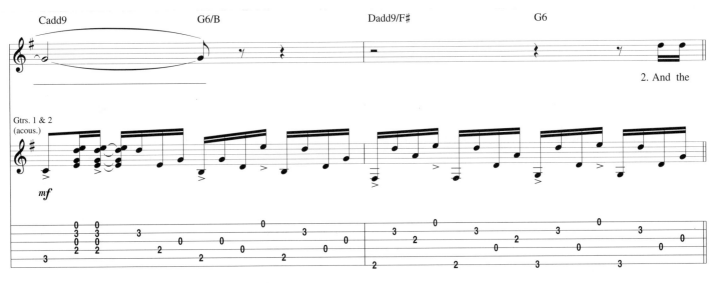

2. And the

Gtrs. 1 & 2
(acous.)

mf

Verse

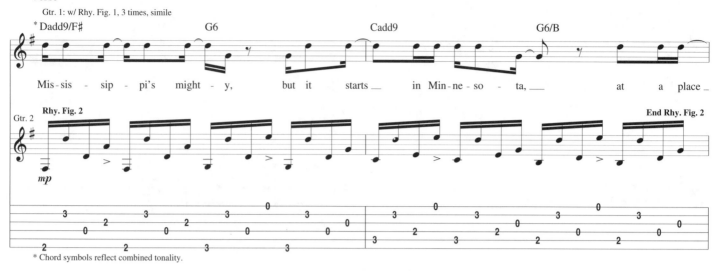

Mis-sis - sip - pi's might - y, but it starts __ in Min-ne-so - ta, __ at a place __

* Chord symbols reflect combined tonality.

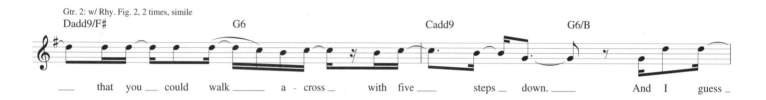

__ that you __ could walk __ a - cross __ with five __ steps __ down. __ And I guess __

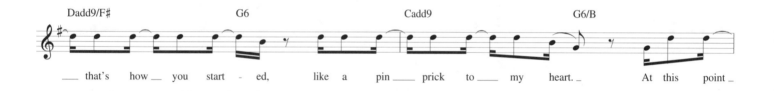

__ that's how __ you start - ed, like a pin __ prick to __ my heart. _ At this point __

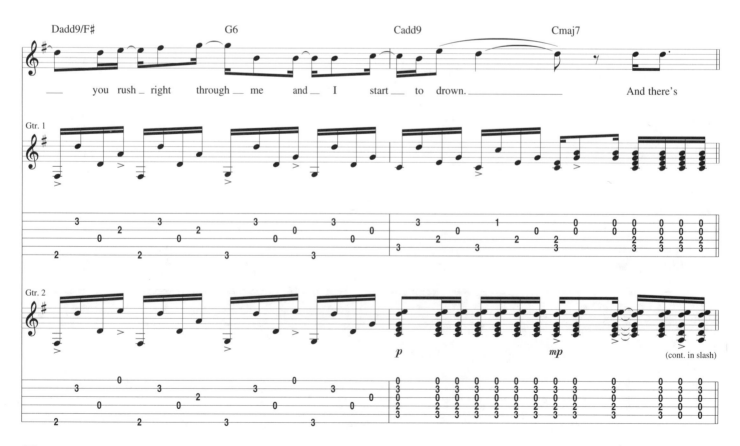

__ you rush __ right through __ me and __ I start __ to drown. _____ And there's

Chorus

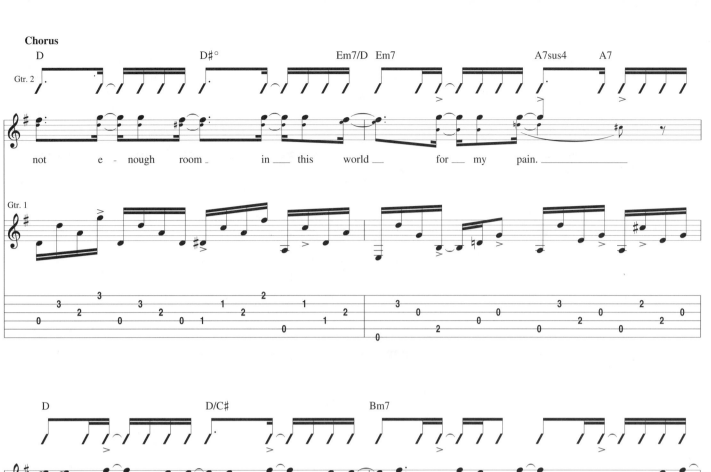

not e - nough room in this world for my pain.

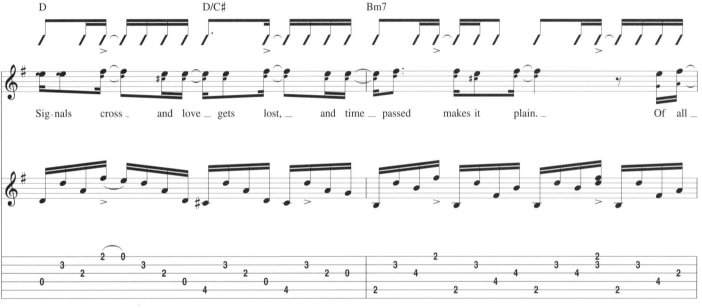

Sig-nals cross and love gets lost, and time passed makes it plain. Of all

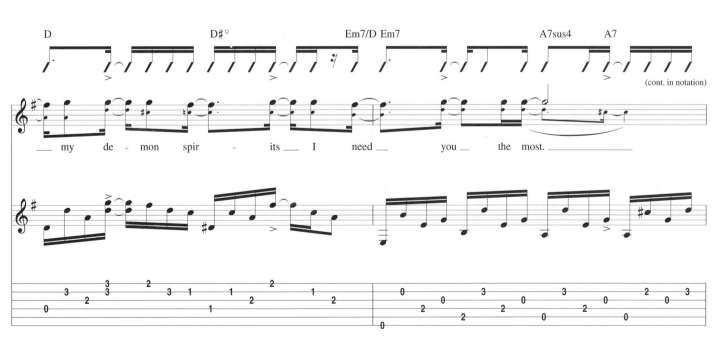

my de - mon spir - its I need you the most.

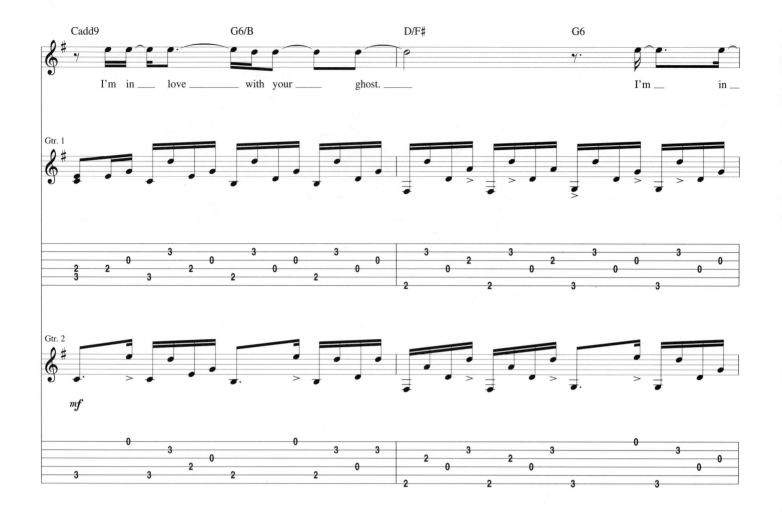

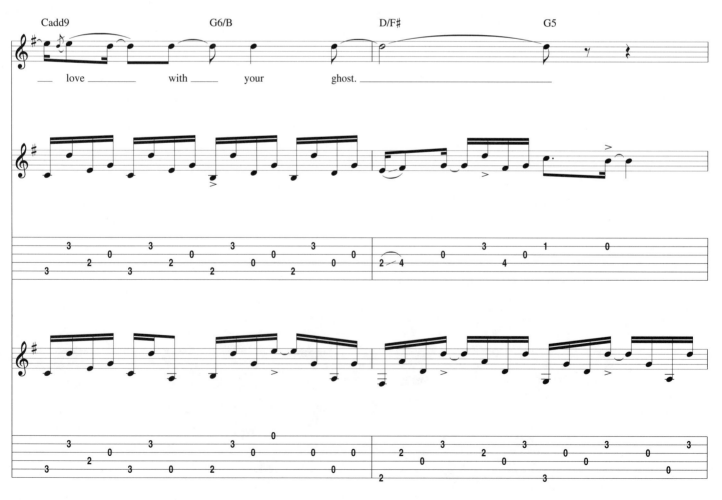

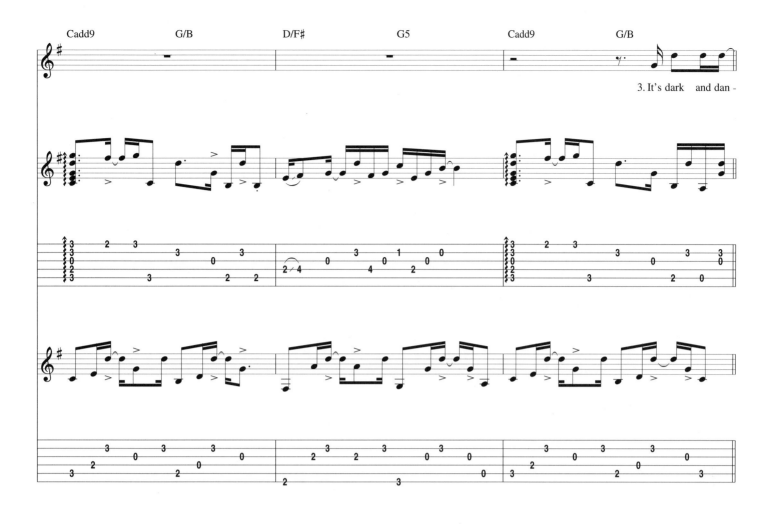

3. It's dark and dan-

Verse

___ g'rous like ___ a sec - ret that gets whis - pered in a hush. ____ When I wake ___
(Don't tell _____ it's soul. ____)

the things I dreamt a - bout you last night make me blush. When you kiss
(Don't tell a soul.)

Rhy. Fig. 3   End Rhy. Fig. 3

Rhy. Fig. 3A   End Rhy. Fig. 3A

Gtrs. 1 & 2: w/ Rhy. Figs. 3 & 3A, simile

me like a lov - er, then you sting me like a vi - per. I go

fol - low to the riv - er, play your mem - or - y like the pip - er. Then I

* Gtrs. 1 & 2

(cont. in slash)

ƒ

* composite arrangement

Chorus

Gtrs.
1 & 2

feel it like a sick - ness, how this love is kill - ing me. But I'd

walk in - to the fin - gers of your fire will - ing - ly. And dance

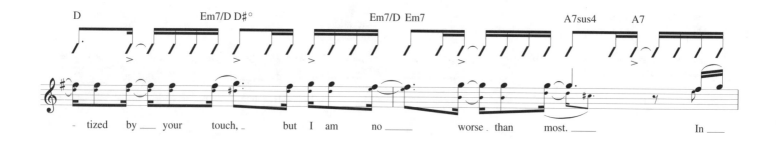

-tized by ___ your touch, ___ but I am no ___ worse . than most. ___ In ___

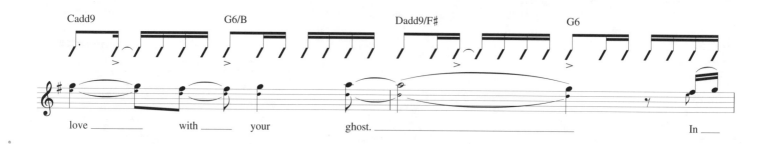

love ___ with ___ your ghost. ___ In ___

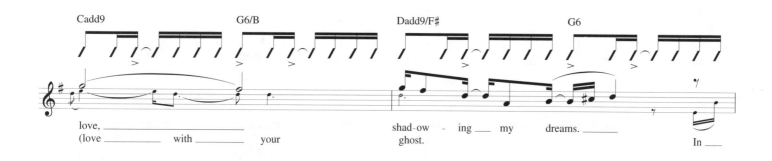

love, ___ (love ___ with ___ your ghost. shad-ow - ing ___ my dreams. ___ In ___

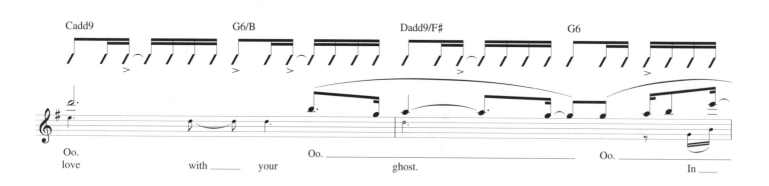

Oo. love with ___ your Oo. ___ ghost. Oo. ___ In ___

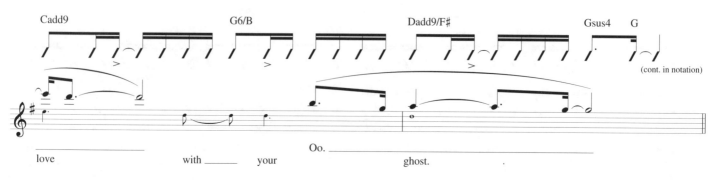

(cont. in notation)

love ___ with ___ your Oo. ___ ghost.

Outro

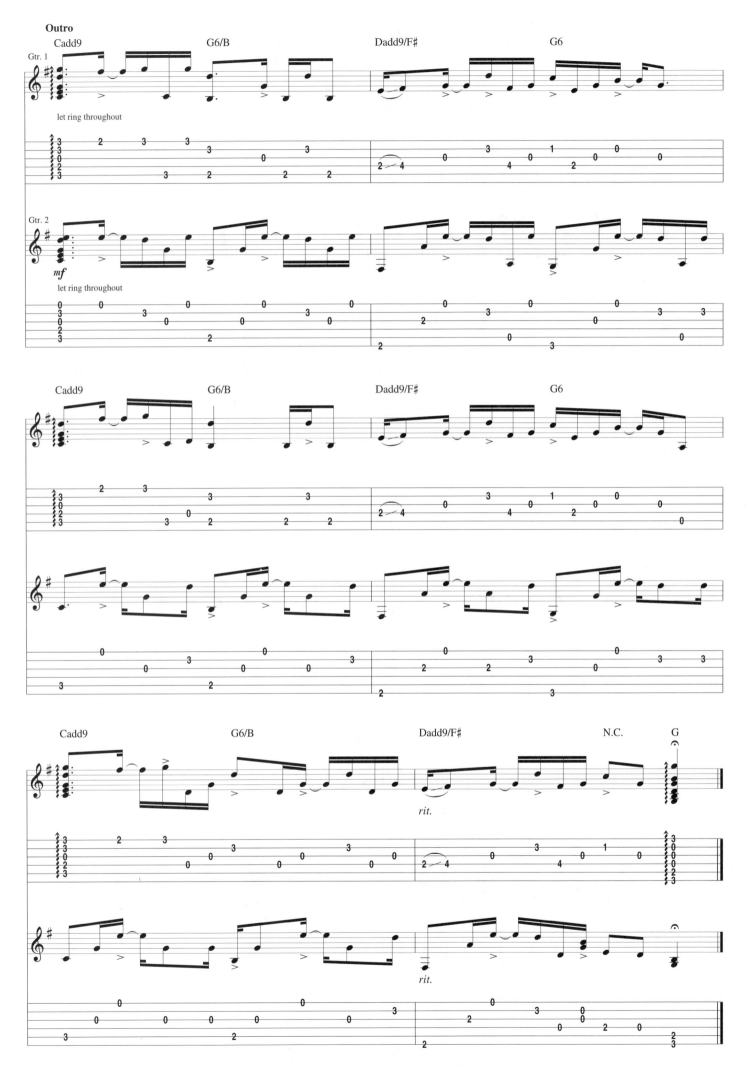

I Don't Wanna Know

Words and Music by Amy Ray and Michelle Malone

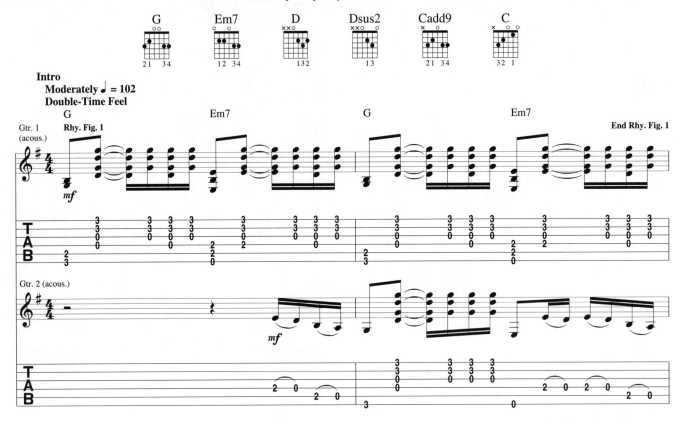

Intro
Moderately ♩ = 102
Double-Time Feel

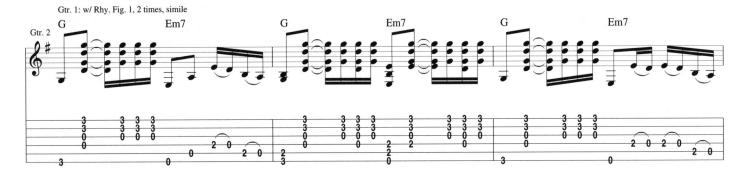

Well, you fol - lowed me __ this far. __ Did you find
__ me all __ your se - crets and I
you know __ the an - swers, you've

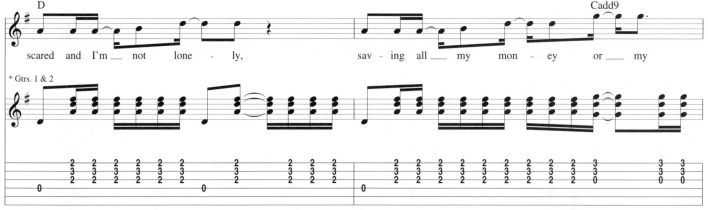

scared and I'm __ not lone - ly, sav - ing all __ my mon - ey or __ my

* Gtrs. 1 & 2

* composite arrangement

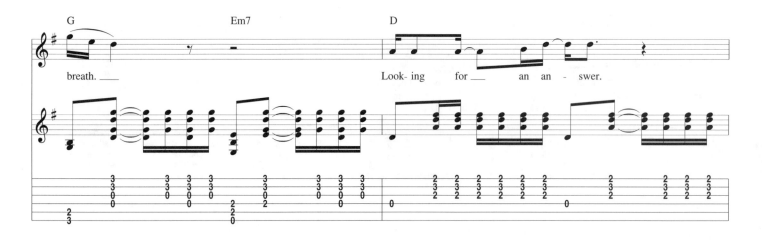

breath. __ Look- ing for __ an an - swer.

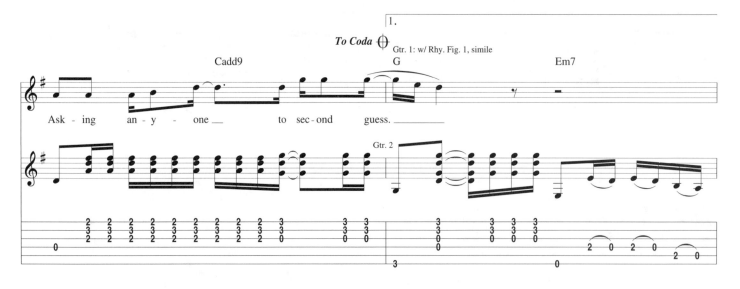

To Coda ⊕   Gtr. 1: w/ Rhy. Fig. 1, simile

Ask - ing an - y - one __ to sec - ond guess. __

Gtr. 2

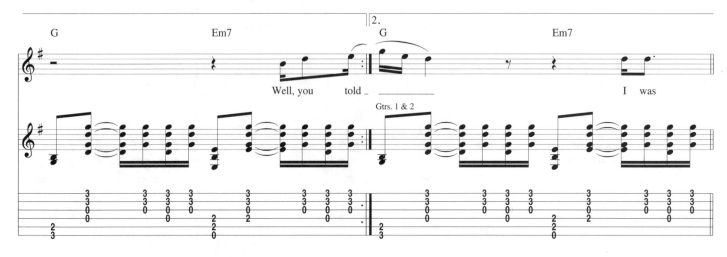

Well, you told __ I was

Gtrs. 1 & 2

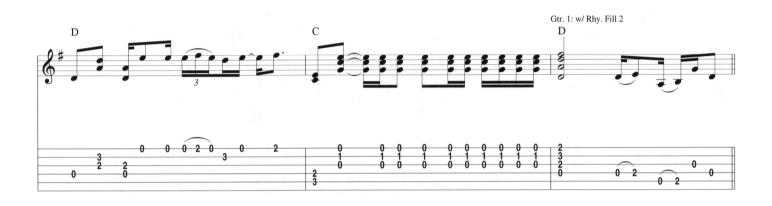

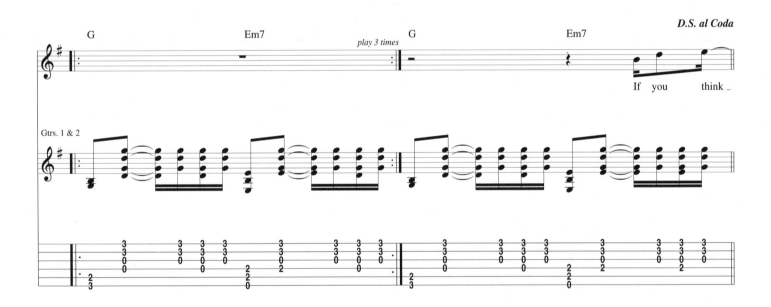

If you   you   think

Joking

Words and Music by Amy Ray

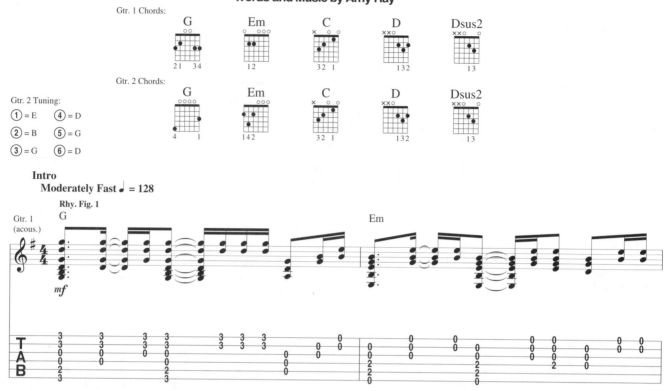

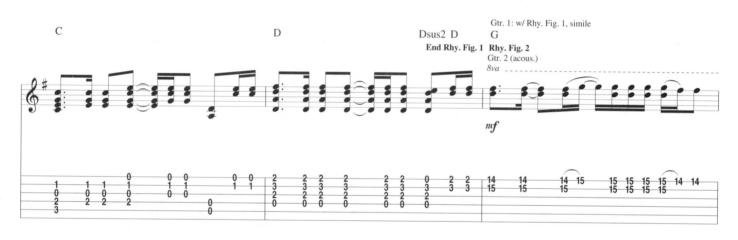

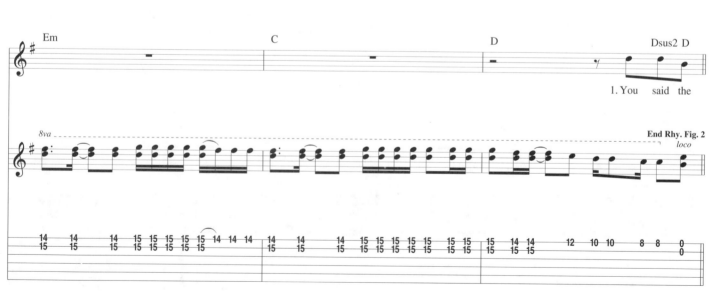

Jonas & Ezekial

Words and Music by Amy Ray

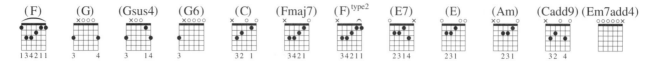

Notes from Amy: This song looks harder than it is – but I'm not going to change the chords provided here because they sound pretty good. Basically, I play basic chords, but I tend to lift different fingers on and off in different places – I don't know how to notate those things because they change everytime we play it...so you can make up your own way or follow this book. A.R.

Gtrs. 1 & 2: Capo II

Verse

Moderately ♩ = 120

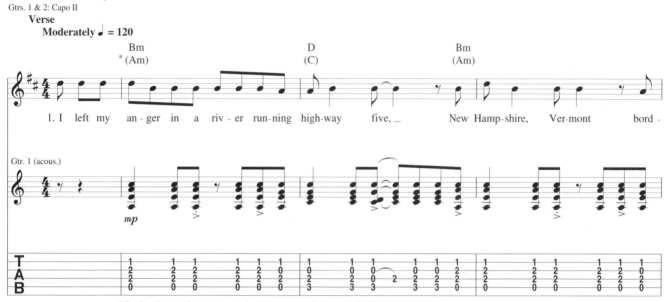

* Symbols in parentheses represent chord names respective to capoed guitars.
Symbols above reflect actual sounding chords. Capoed fret is "0" in TAB.

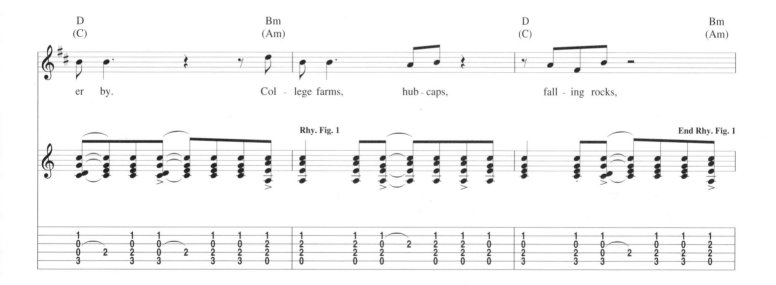

Gtr. 1: w/ Rhy. Fig. 1, 4 times, simile

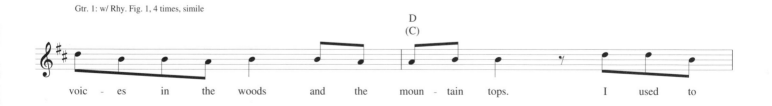

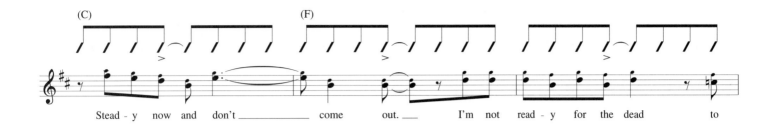

Stead - y now and don't _____ come out. ___ I'm not read - y for the dead to

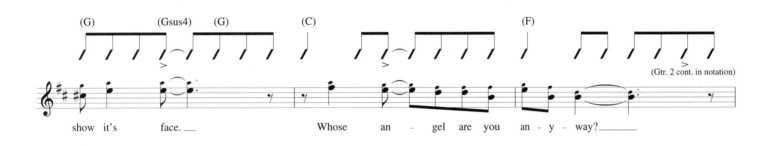

show it's face. ___ Whose an - gel are you an - y - way? _____

Interlude

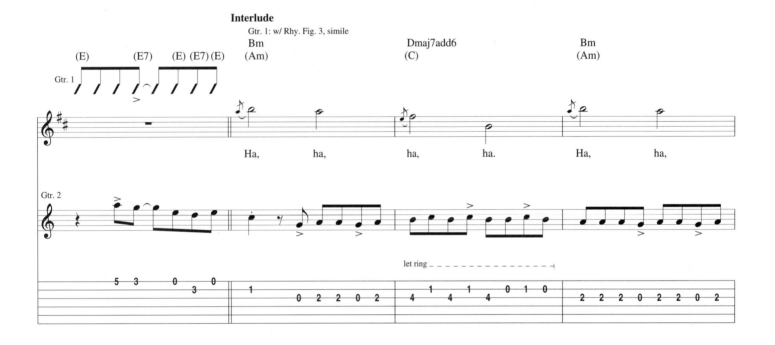

Gtr. 1: w/ Rhy. Fig. 3, simile

Ha, ha, ha, ha. Ha, ha,

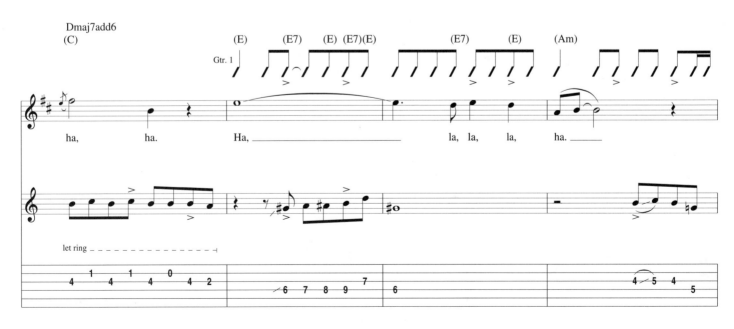

ha, ha. Ha, _____ la, la, la, ha. ___

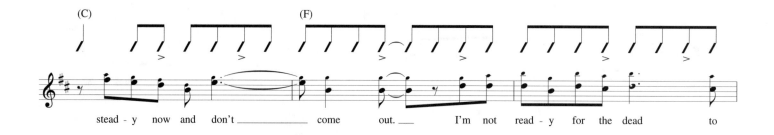

stead - y now and don't _____ come out. ___ I'm not read - y for the dead to

show it's face. ___ Whose ___ turn ___ is it an - y - way? I said,

Chorus

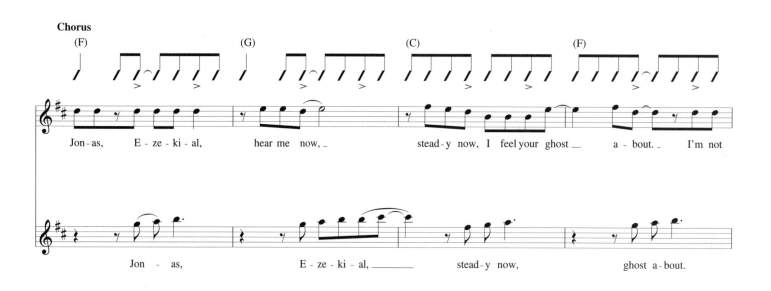

Jon - as, E - ze - ki - al, hear me now, _ stead - y now, I feel your ghost ___ a - bout. _ I'm not

Jon - as, E - ze - ki - al, _____ stead - y now, ghost a - bout.

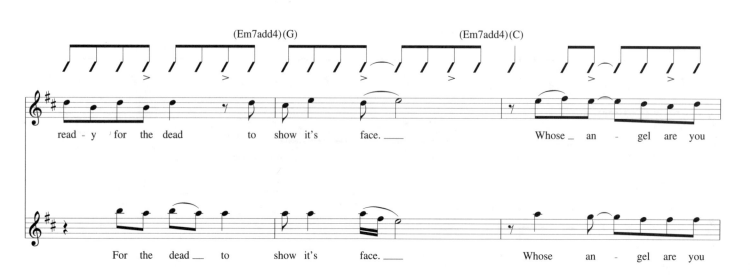

read - y for the dead to show it's face. ___ Whose _ an - gel are you

For the dead ___ to show it's face. ___ Whose an - gel are you

Least Complicated

Words and Music by Emily Saliers

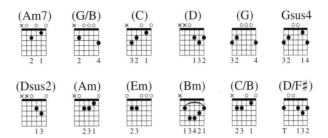

Gtr. 2: Capo II

Intro

Moderately Fast ♩ = 102

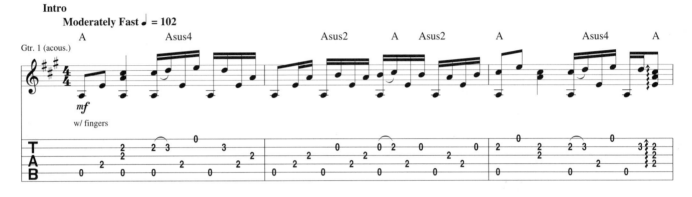

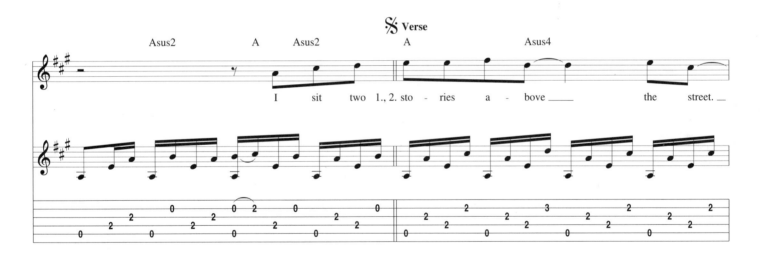

I sit two 1., 2. sto - ries a - bove _____ the street. _____

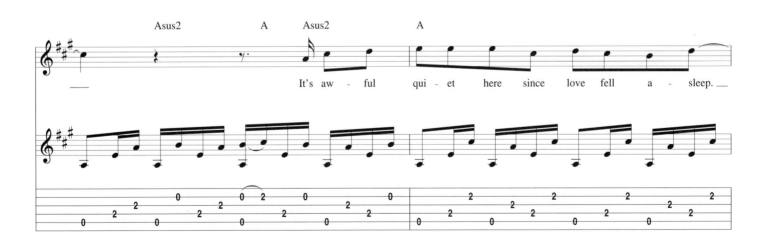

_____ It's aw - ful qui - et here since love fell a - sleep. _____

* Symbols in parentheses represent chord names respective to capoed guitar and do not reflect actual sounding chord.

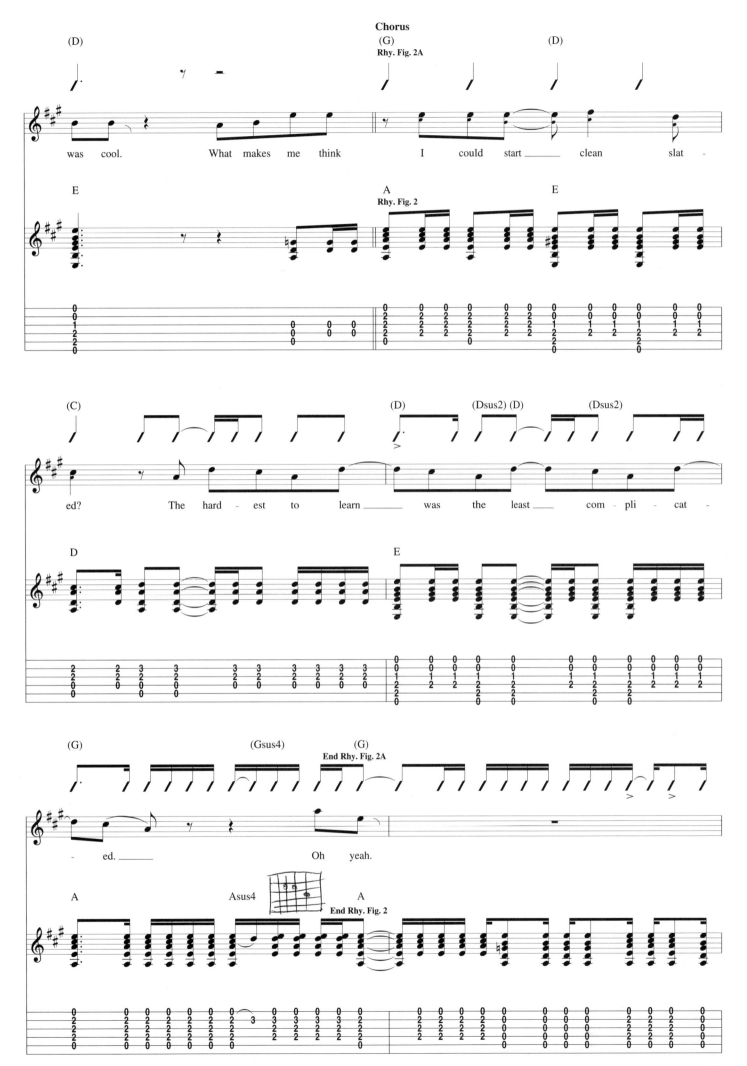

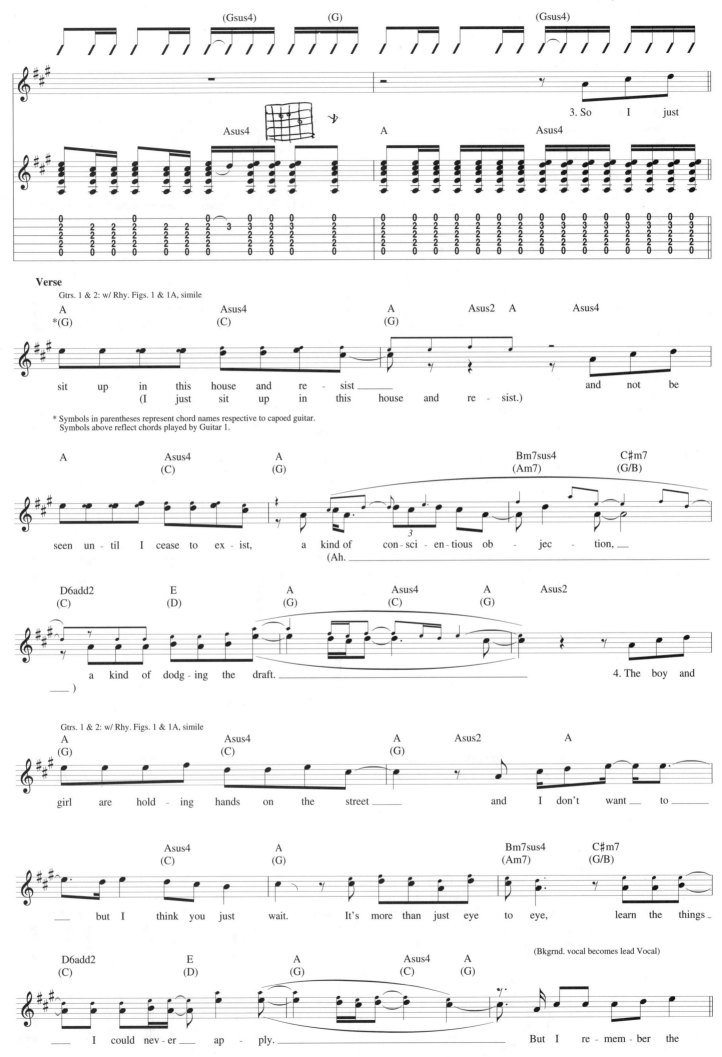

Chorus

I could start ___ clean slat - ed? The hard - est to learn ___ was the least ___ com - pli - cat -

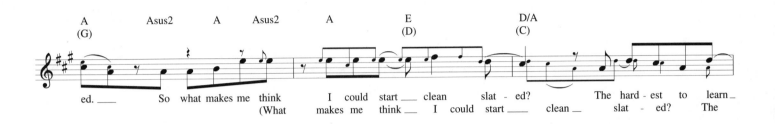

ed. ___ So what makes me think I could start ___ clean slat - ed? The hard - est to learn ___
(What makes me think ___ I could start ___ clean ___ slat - ed? The

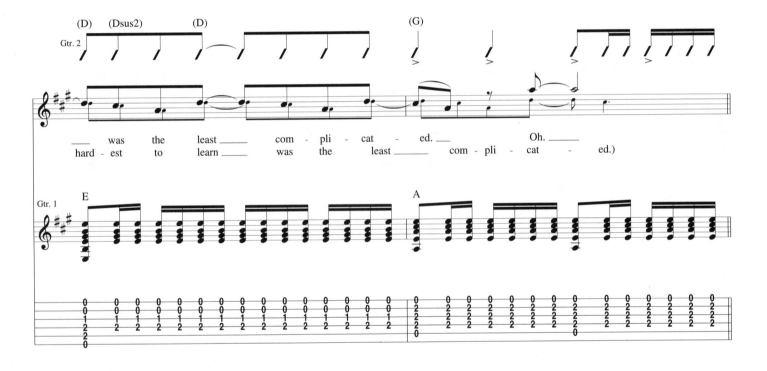

___ was the least ___ com - pli - cat - ed. ___ Oh. ___
hard - est to learn ___ was the least ___ com - pli - cat - ed.)

Bridge

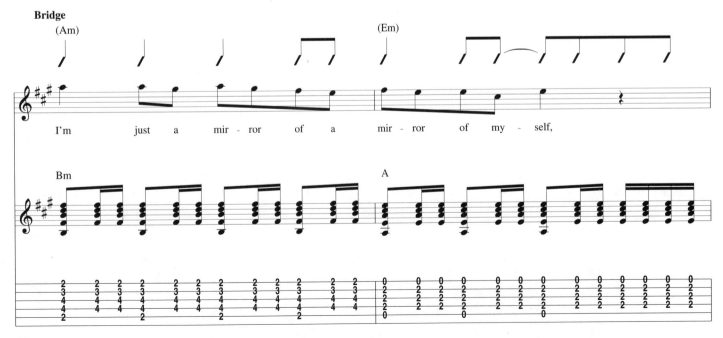

I'm just a mir - ror of a mir - ror of my - self,

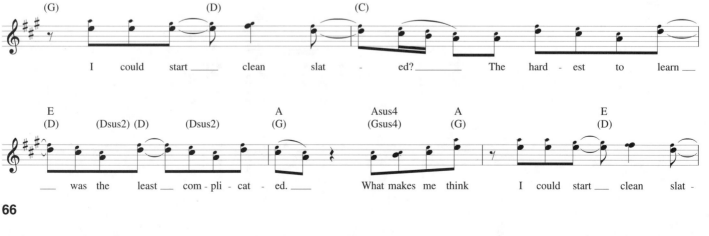

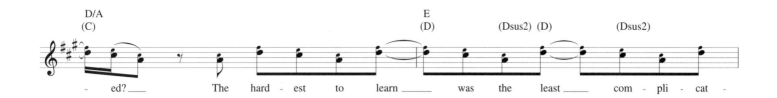

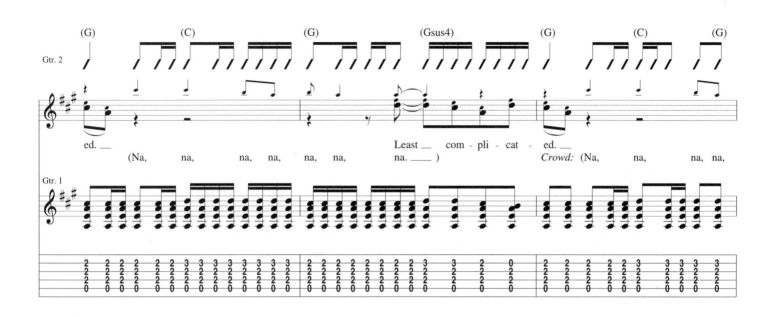

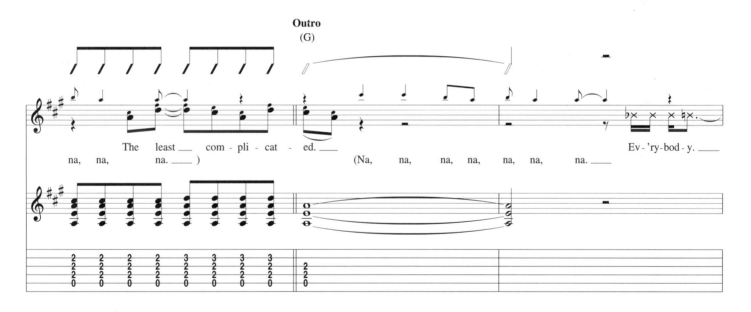

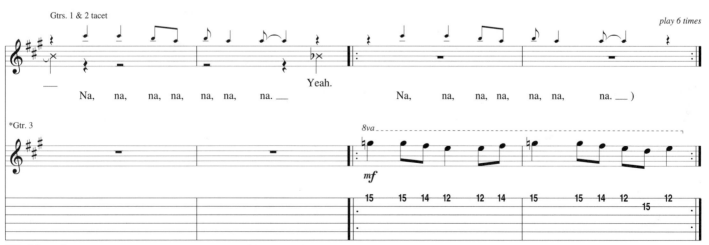

* Mandolin arr. for gtr.

Mystery

Words and Music by Emily Saliers

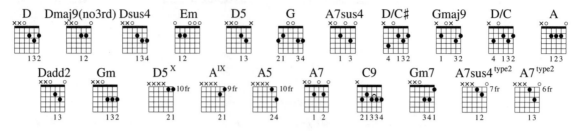

Gtr. 1; Tuning:
① = D   ④ = D
② = A   ⑤ = A
③ = G   ⑥ = D

Amy's part (Gtr. 2) was played on a high-strung guitar. This is a trick used widely to add another texture to the song. String a 6-string with smaller gauges and tune it an octave up.

Intro

Moderately Slow ♩. = 50

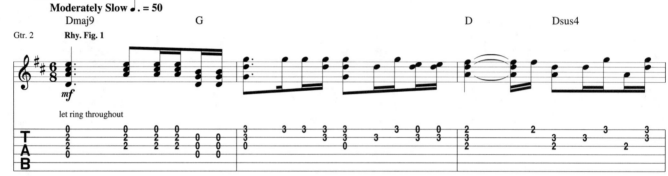

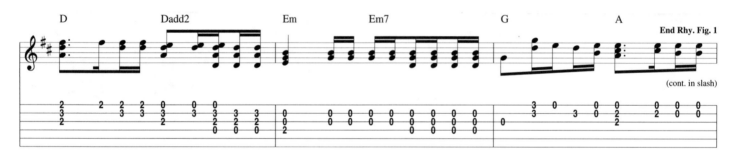

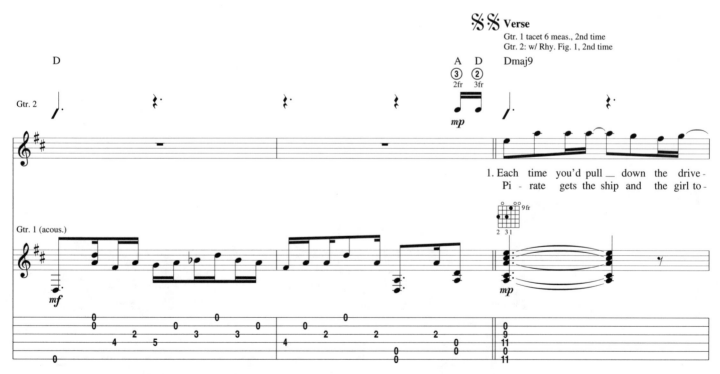

- and things ___ you would die ___ for,
- and things ___ you would die ___ for.)
well I can hard - ly ___ think of __ two

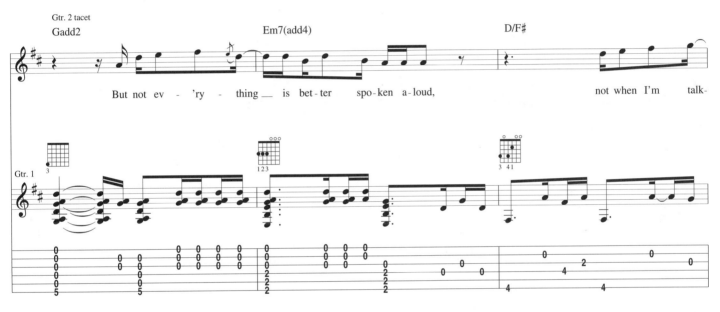

Gtr. 2 tacet

But not ev - 'ry - thing ___ is bet - ter spo-ken a-loud,   not when I'm talk-

D.S.S. al Coda 2

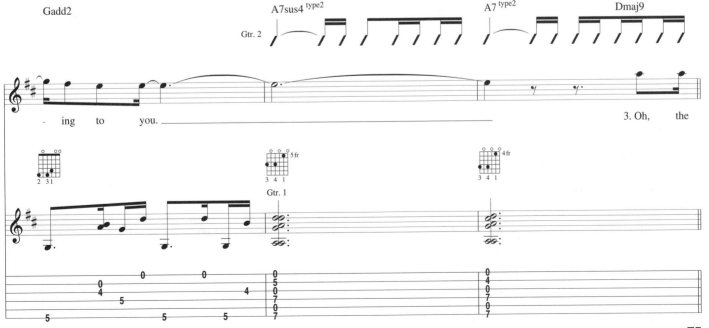

- ing to you. ___   3. Oh, the

Power of Two

Words and Music by Emily Saliers

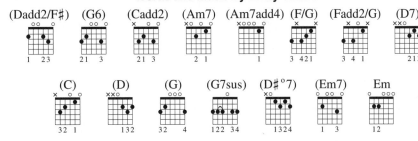

Gtrs. 1 & 2: Capo V

Intro
Moderately ♩ = 122
N.C.

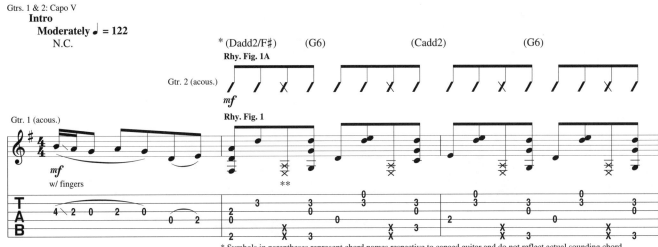

* Symbols in parentheses represent chord names respective to capoed guitar and do not reflect actual sounding chord.
Capoed fret is "0" in TAB.
** Slap right hand thumb on the 5th and 6th strings.

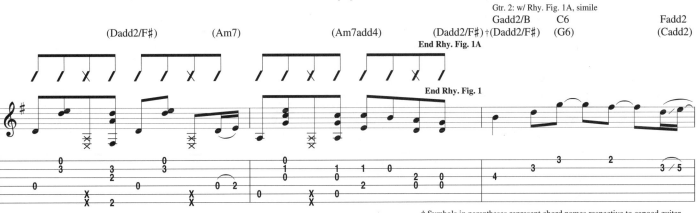

† Symbols in parentheses represent chord names respective to capoed guitar.
Symbols above reflect actual sounding chord.

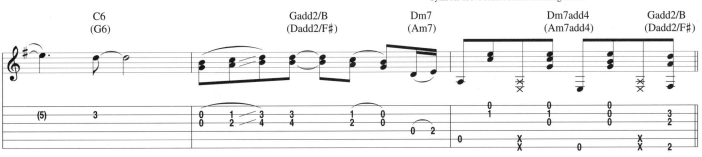

Verse

Gtrs. 1 & 2: w/ Rhy. Figs. 1 & 1A

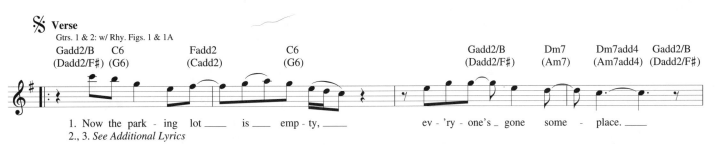

1. Now the park - ing lot ____ is ____ emp - ty, ____ ev - 'ry - one's _ gone some - place. ____
2., 3. *See Additional Lyrics*

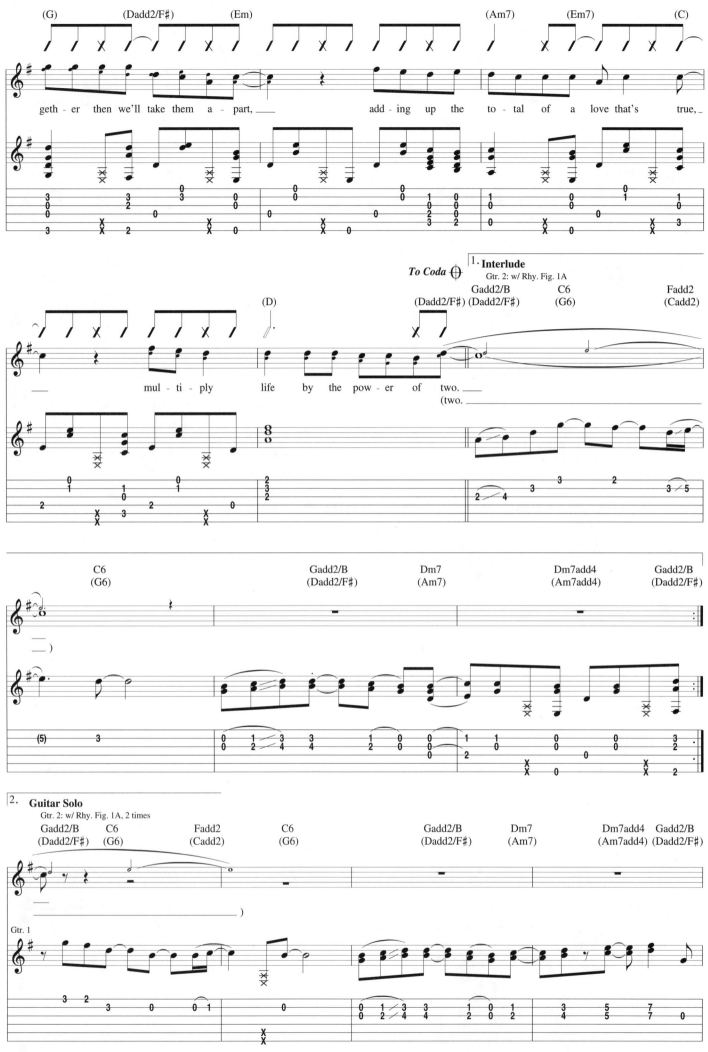

Additional Lyrics

2. You know the things that I am afraid of,
   I'm not afraid to tell.
   And if we'd ever leave a legacy,
   It's that we loved each other well.
   Because I've seen the shadows of so many people,
   Still trying on the treasures of youth.
   But a road that fancy and fast ends in a fatal crash
   And I'm glad we got off, to tell you the truth.

3. And now we're talking about a difficult thing
   And your eyes are getting wet.
   But I took us for better and I took us for worse
   And don't you ever forget it. (And now the steel bars.)
   The steel bars between me and a promise,
   They suddenly bend with ease.
   The closer I'm bound in love to you
   The closer I am to free.

Pushing the Needle Too Far

Words and Music by Amy Ray

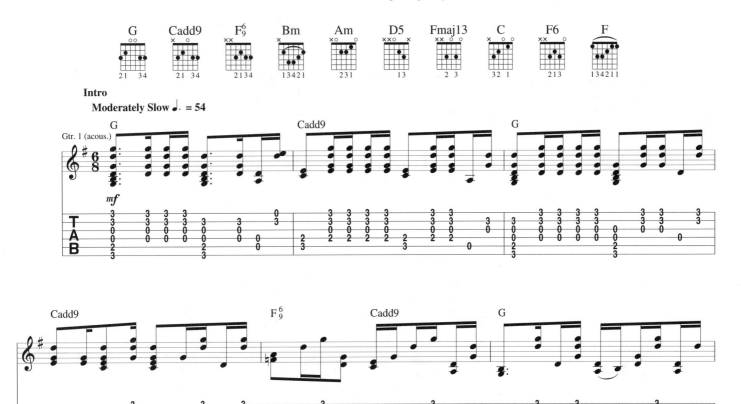

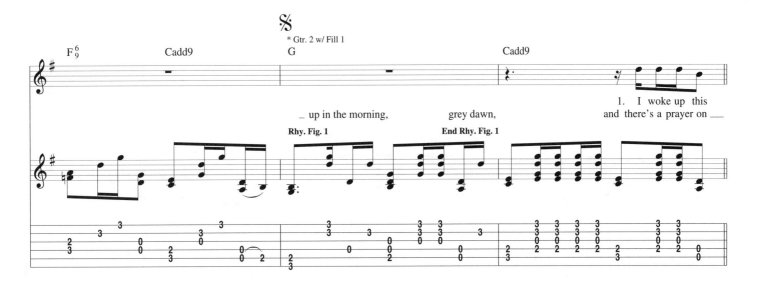

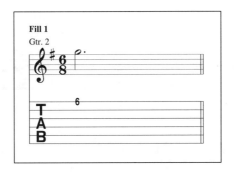

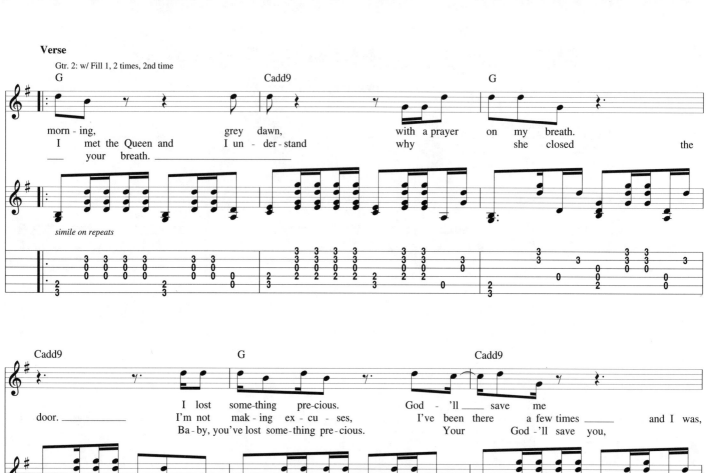

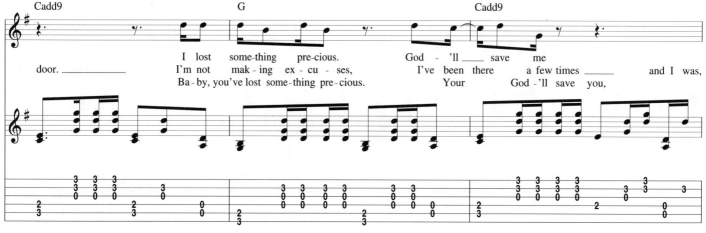

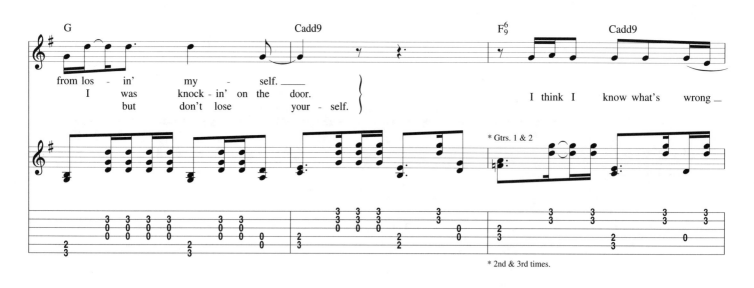

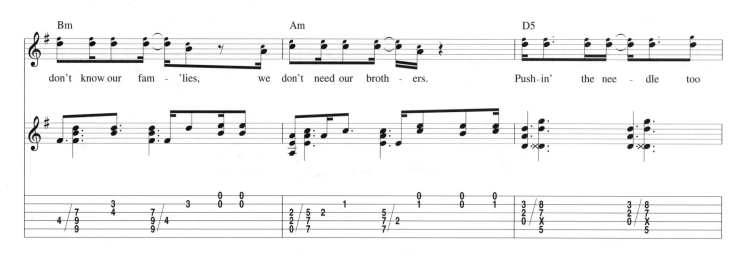

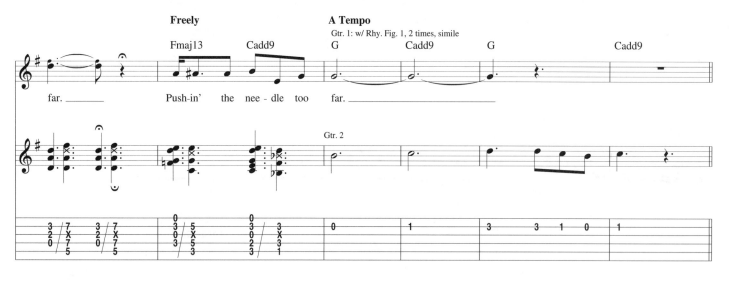

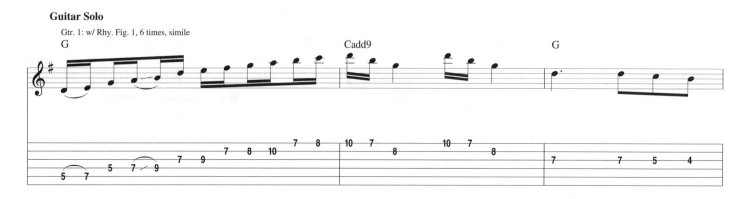

D.S. al Coda

Well,   if you wake

⊕ *Coda*

Outro

w/ ad Lib vocs., 2nd and 3rd times:

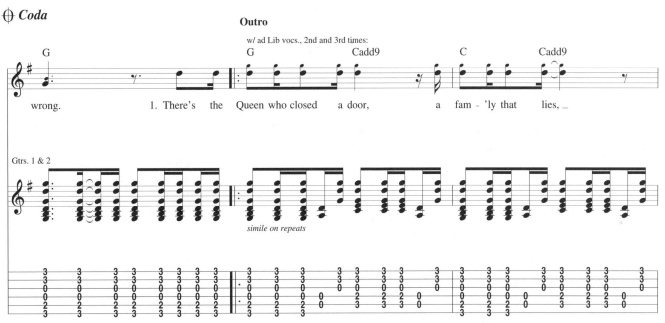

wrong.   1. There's   the   Queen who closed   a door,   a   fam - 'ly that   lies,

Gtrs. 1 & 2

simile on repeats

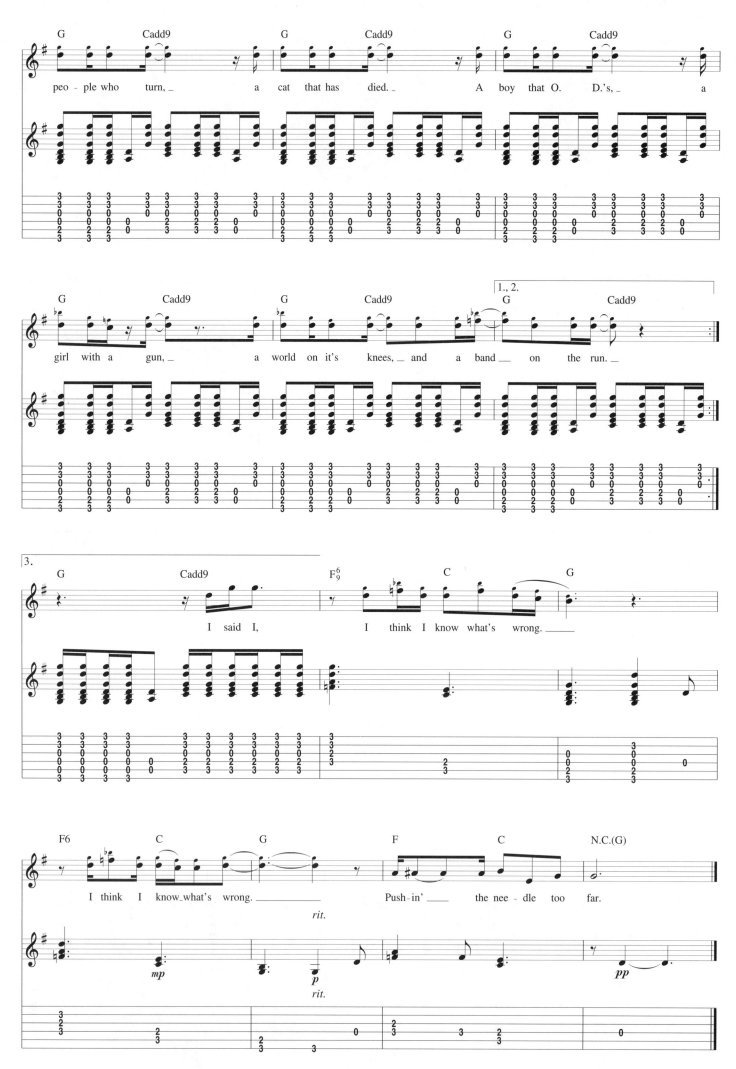

Strange Fire

Words and Music by Amy Ray

1. I come to you with strange fire. I make an
2. Mer-ce-nar-ies of the shrine, now, who are
3. When you learn to love your-self, you will dis-

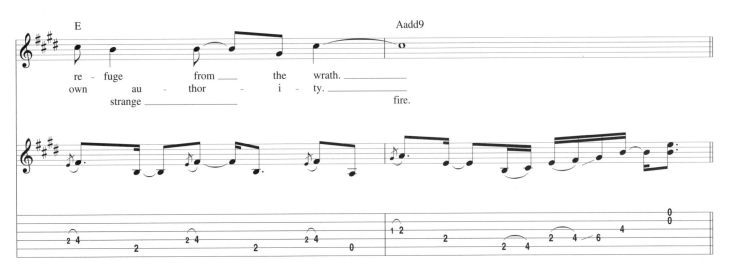

Chorus

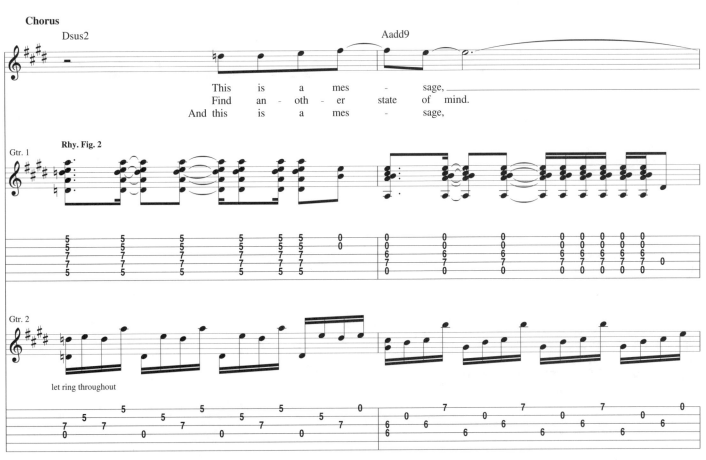

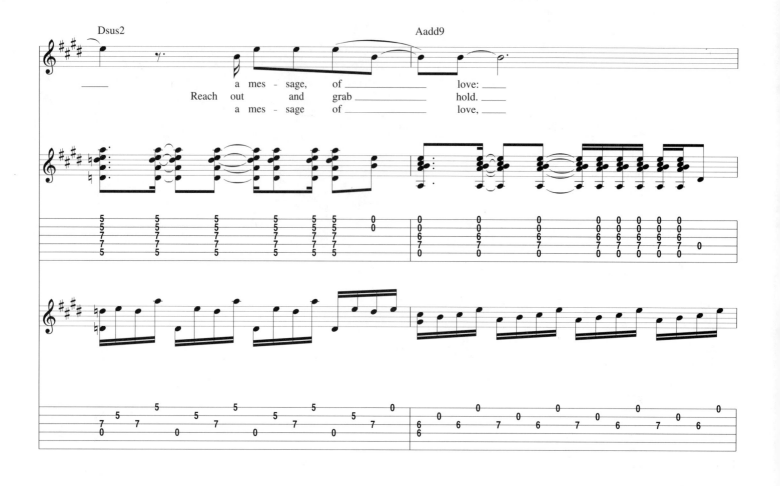

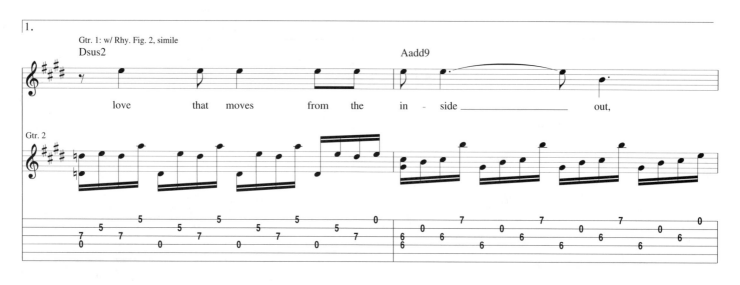

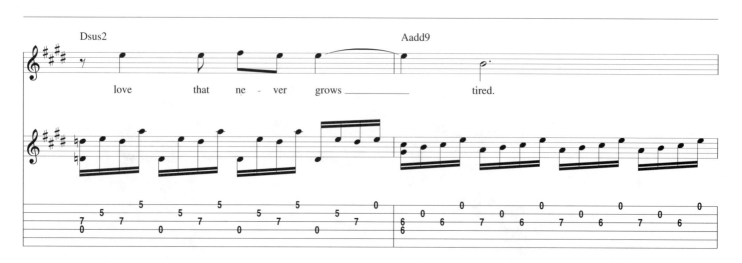

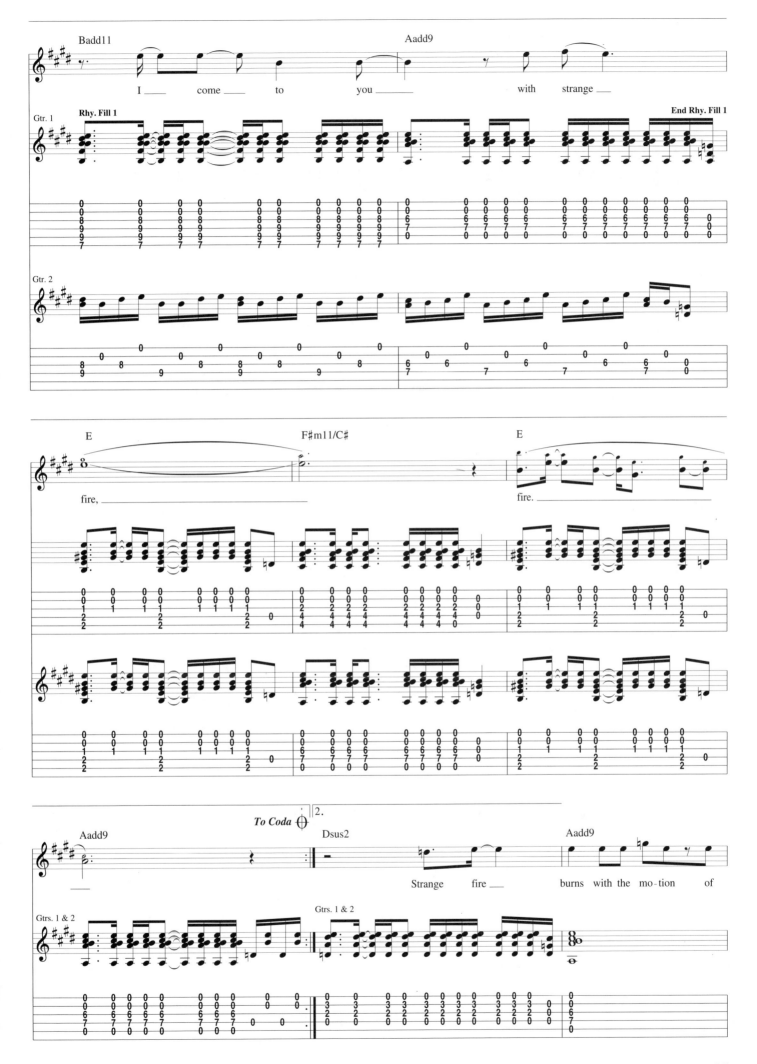

This Train Revised

Words and Music by Amy Ray

Notes from Amy: The beginning section is improv. – I can't be sure it's right, I don't remember what I said or played...you can follow this or create your own. A.R.

Emily's guitar part is played on Dobro with a slide.

* Symbols in parentheses represent chord names respective to capoed guitar.
Symbols above reflect actual sounding chord. Capoed fret is "0" in TAB.

* Played behind the beat.

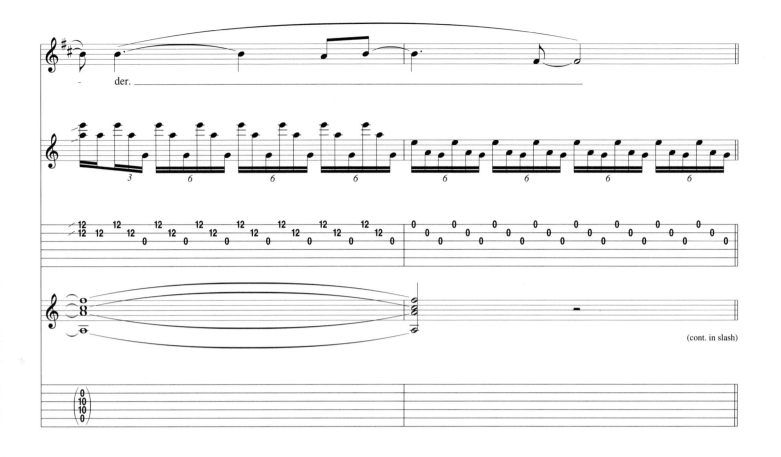

Interlude
Faster ♩ = 140

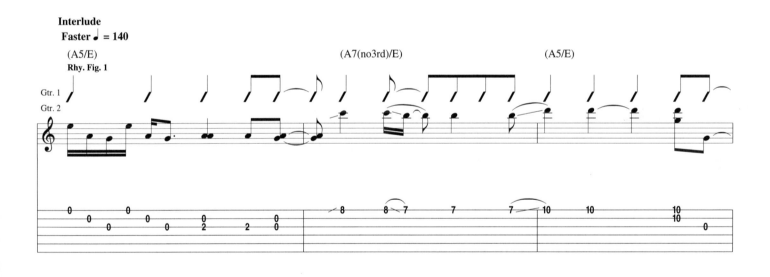

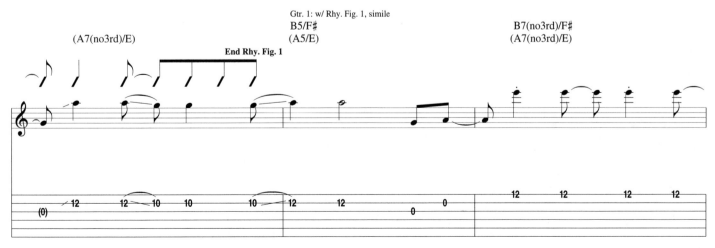

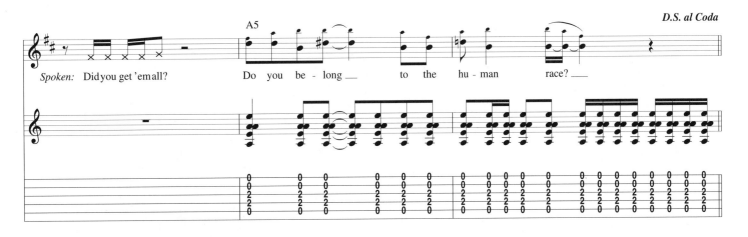

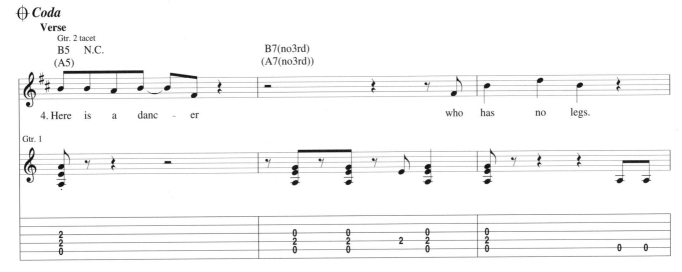

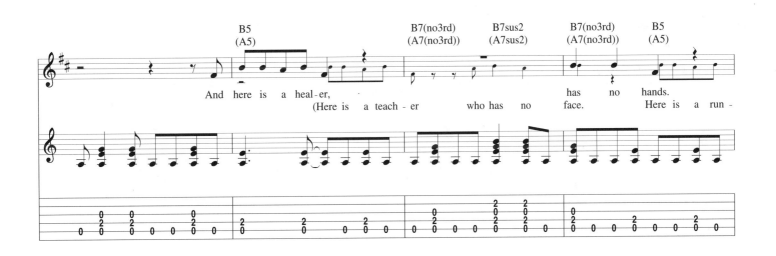

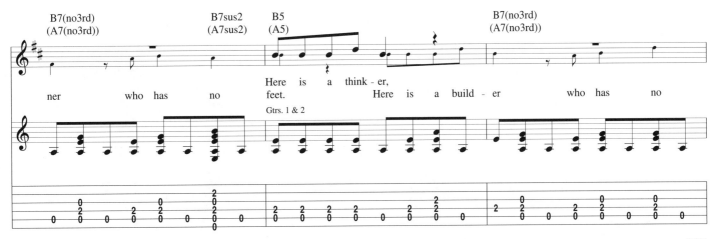

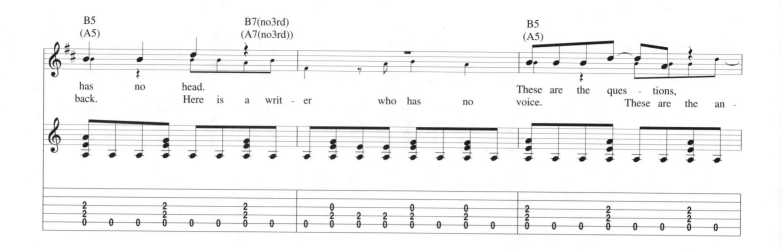

has no head.
back.   Here is a writ-er   who has   no   These are the ques-tions,
voice.   These are the an-

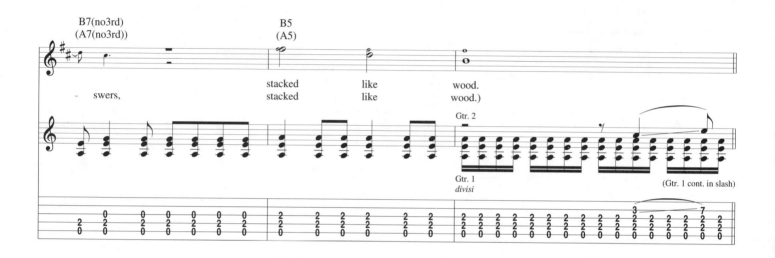

-swers,
stacked   like   wood.
stacked   like   wood.)

Guitar Solo

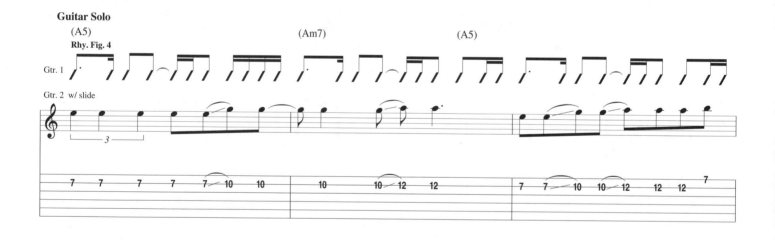

Gtr. 1: w/ Rhy. Fig. 4, 3 times, simile

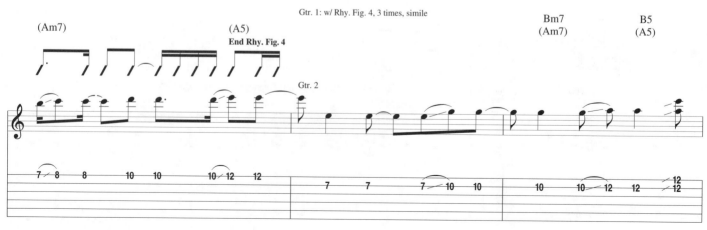

Virginia Woolf

Words and Music by Emily Saliers

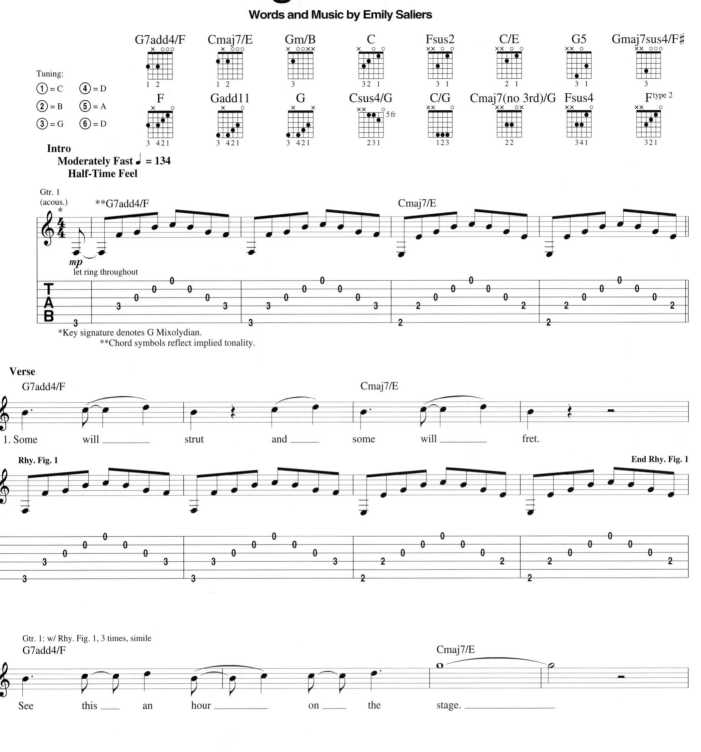

*Key signature denotes G Mixolydian.
**Chord symbols reflect implied tonality.

Verse

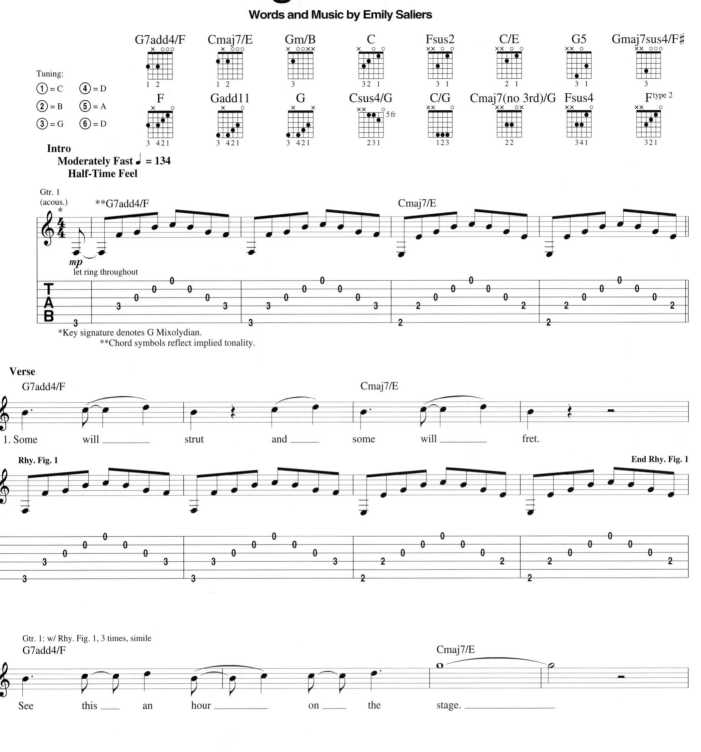

1. Some will _____ strut and _____ some will _____ fret.

See this ____ an hour _____ on ____ the stage. _____

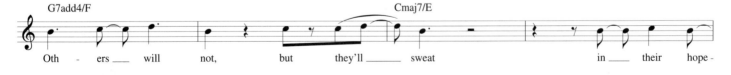

Oth - ers _____ will not, but they'll _____ sweat in ____ their hope -

- less - ness, _____ in ____ their rage. _____ We're all the same, __

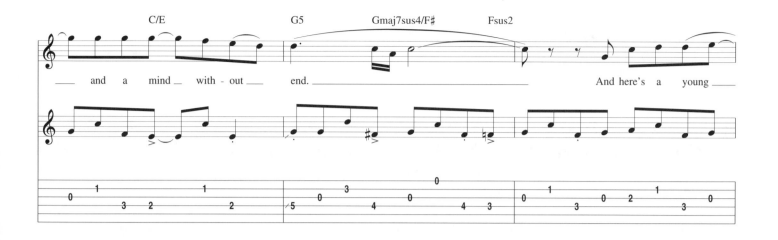

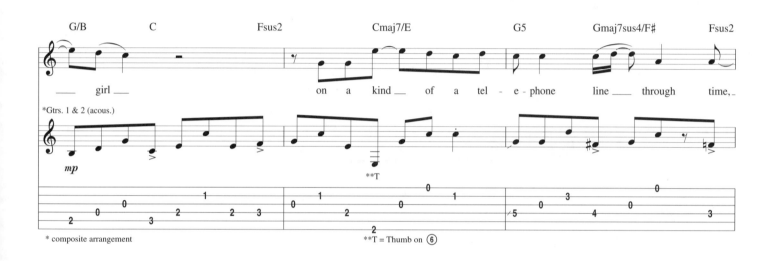

* composite arrangement   **T = Thumb on ⑥

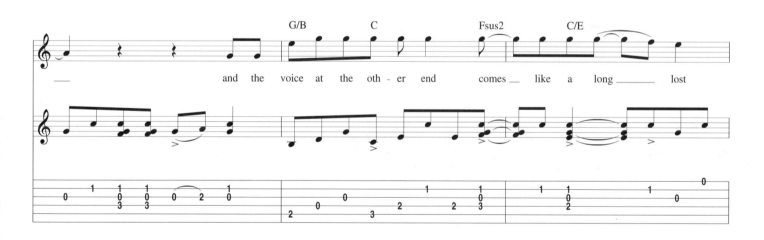

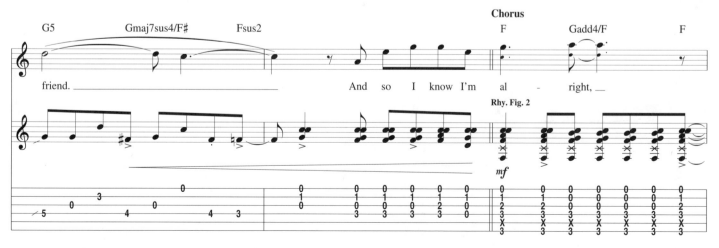

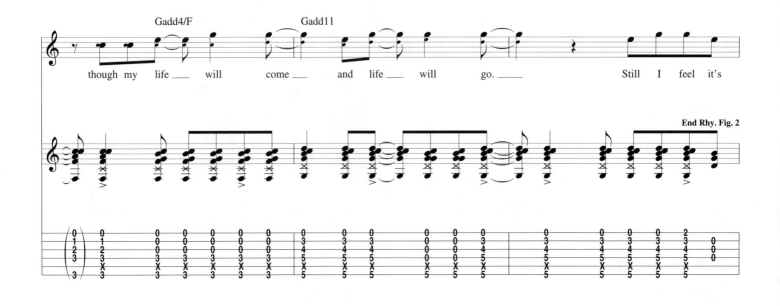

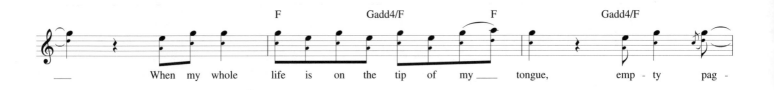

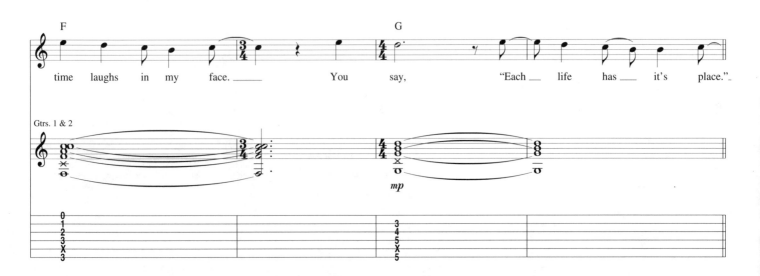

Interlude

Yeah.

3. The hatch - es were _____ bat - tened, _

Verse

113

the thun-der clouds rolled and the crit - ics stormed. _____ The

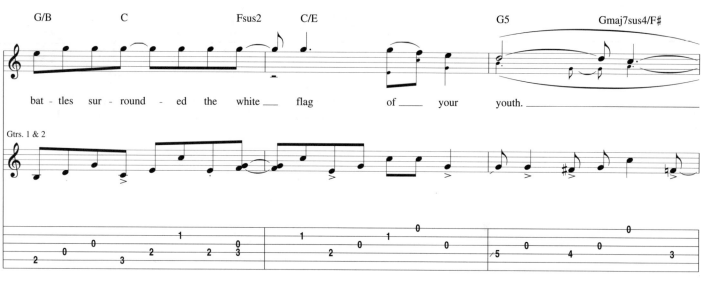

bat - tles sur - round - ed the white ___ flag of ___ your youth. _____

_____ But, if you need to know that you weath-ered the storm ___ of cruel ___ mor -

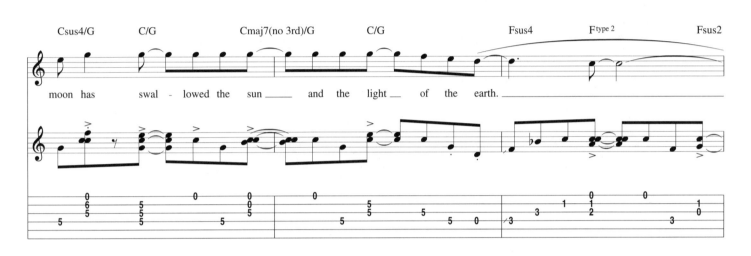

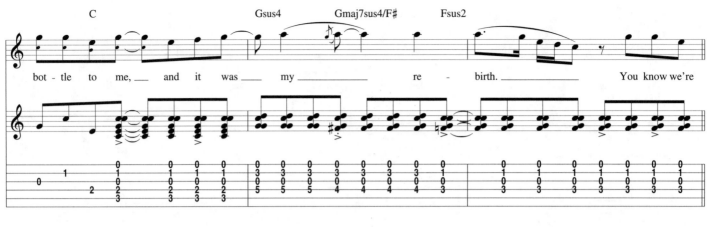

Chorus

Gtrs. 1 & 2: w/ Rhy. Fig. 2, 5 times, simile

World Falls

Words and Music by Amy Ray

Gtrs. 1 & 2: Capo III

Intro

Moderately Fast ♩ = 140

* Symbols in parentheses represent chord names respective to capoed guitars. Symbols above reflect actual sounding chords.
Capoed fret is "0" in TAB. Chord symbols reflect combined tonality.

Gtr. 2: w/ Rhy. Fig. 1, simile

1. I'm

𝄋 Verse

Gtr. 2: w/ Rhy. Fig. 1, 4 times, simile
Gtr. 1: w/ Fill 1, 2nd time

simile on repeats

com - ing home ___ with a stone ___ strapped on to my back. ___
I woke up in the mid - dle of a dream, ___ I was scared the world was too
3. Wish I was ___ a No - mad, _____ an In - di - an or a Saint. ___

121

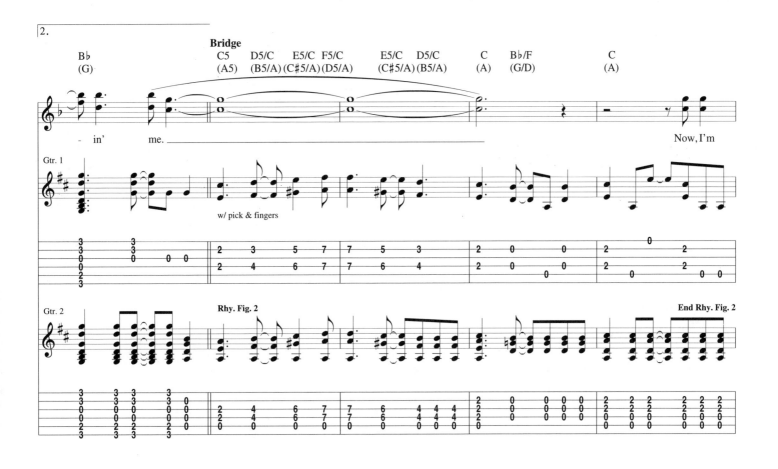

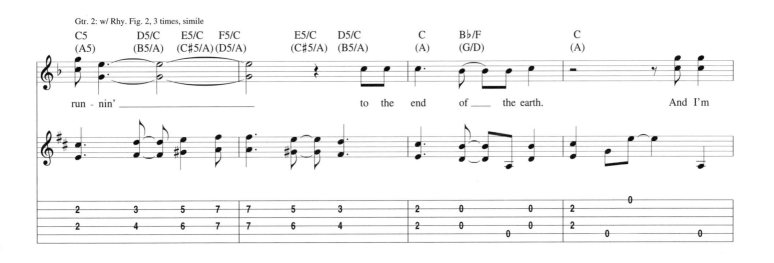

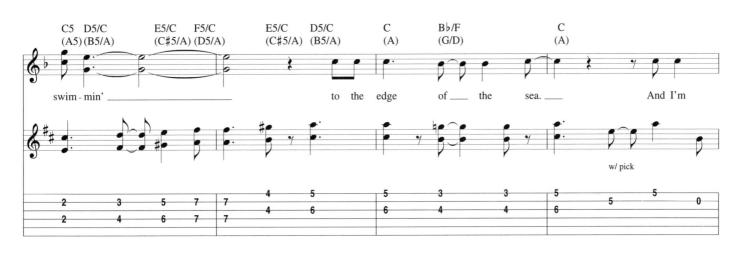

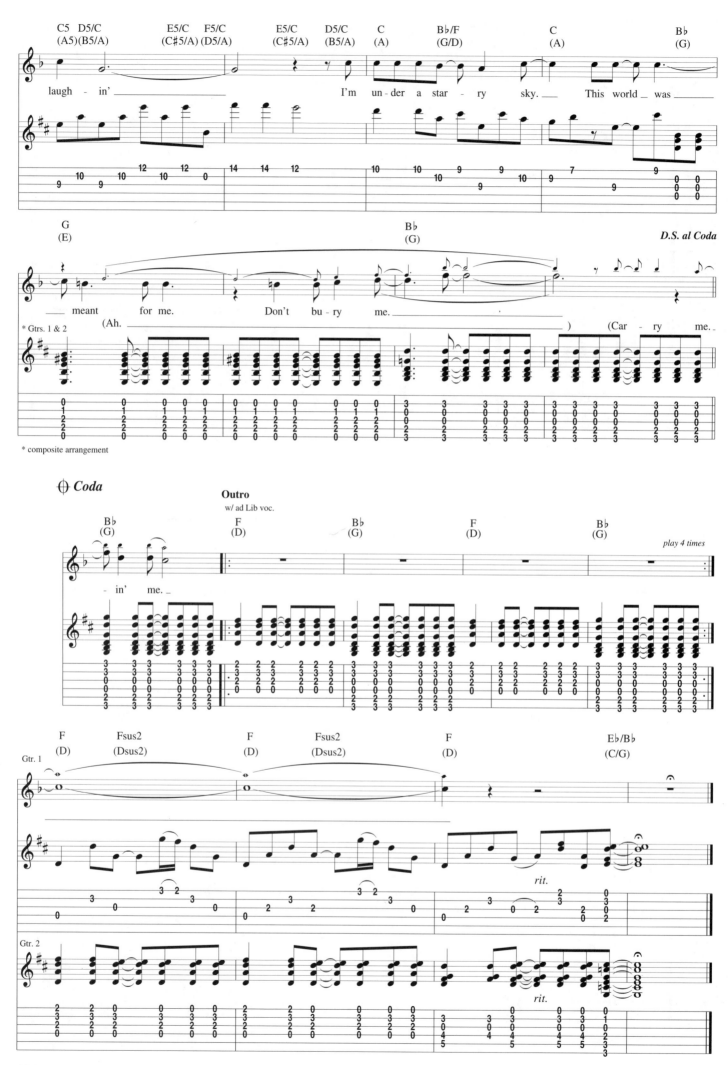

Guitar Notation Legend

Guitar Music can be notated three different ways: on a *musical staff*, in *tablature*, and in *rhythm slashes*.

RHYTHM SLASHES are written above the staff. Strum chords in the rhythm indicated. Use the chord diagrams found at the top of the first page of the transcription for the appropriate chord voicings. Round noteheads indicate single notes.

THE MUSICAL STAFF shows pitches and rhythms and is divided by bar lines into measures. Pitches are named after the first seven letters of the alphabet.

TABLATURE graphically represents the guitar fingerboard. Each horizontal line represents a a string, and each number represents a fret.

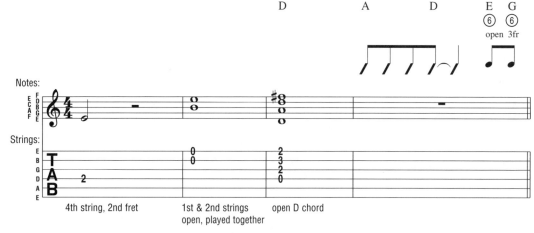

4th string, 2nd fret

1st & 2nd strings open, played together

open D chord

Definitions for Special Guitar Notation

HALF-STEP BEND: Strike the note and bend up 1/2 step.

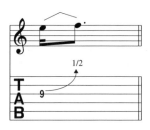

WHOLE-STEP BEND: Strike the note and bend up one step.

GRACE NOTE BEND: Strike the note and bend up as indicated. The first note does not take up any time.

SLIGHT (MICROTONE) BEND: Strike the note and bend up 1/4 step.

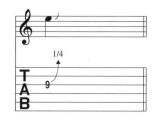

BEND AND RELEASE: Strike the note and bend up as indicated, then release back to the original note. Only the first note is struck.

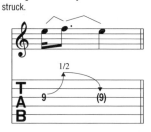

PRE-BEND: Bend the note as indicated, then strike it.

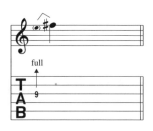

PRE-BEND AND RELEASE: Bend the note as indicated. Strike it and release the bend back to the original note.

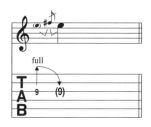

UNISON BEND: Strike the two notes simultaneously and bend the lower note up to the pitch of the higher.

VIBRATO: The string is vibrated by rapidly bending and releasing the note with the fretting hand.

WIDE VIBRATO: The pitch is varied to a greater degree by vibrating with the fretting hand.

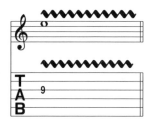

HAMMER-ON: Strike the first (lower) note with one finger, then sound the higher note (on the same string) with another finger by fretting it without picking.

PULL-OFF: Place both fingers on the notes to be sounded. Strike the first note and without picking, pull the finger off to sound the second (lower) note.

LEGATO SLIDE: Strike the first note and then slide the same fret-hand finger up or down to the second note. The second note is not struck.

SHIFT SLIDE: Same as legato slide, except the second note is struck.

TRILL: Very rapidly alternate between the notes indicated by continuously hammering on and pulling off.

TAPPING: Hammer ("tap") the fret indicated with the pick-hand index or middle finger and pull off to the note fretted by the fret hand.

NATURAL HARMONIC: Strike the note while the fret-hand lightly touches the string directly over the fret indicated.

PINCH HARMONIC: The note is fretted normally and a harmonic is produced by adding the edge of the thumb or the tip of the index finger of the pick hand to the normal pick attack.

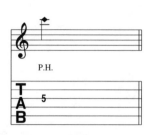

HARP HARMONIC: The note is fretted normally and a harmonic is produced by gently resting the pick hand's index finger directly above the indicated fret (in parentheses) while the pick hand's thumb or pick assists by plucking the appropriate string.

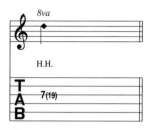

PICK SCRAPE: The edge of the pick is rubbed down (or up) the string, producing a scratchy sound.

MUFFLED STRINGS: A percussive sound is produced by laying the fret hand across the string(s) without depressing, and striking them with the pick hand.

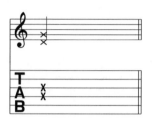

PALM MUTING: The note is partially muted by the pick hand lightly touching the string(s) just before the bridge.

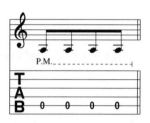

RAKE: Drag the pick across the strings indicated with a single motion.

TREMOLO PICKING: The note is picked as rapidly and continuously as possible.

ARPEGGIATE: Play the notes of the chord indicated by quickly rolling them from bottom to top.

VIBRATO BAR DIVE AND RETURN: The pitch of the note or chord is dropped a specified number of steps (in rhythm) then returned to the original pitch.

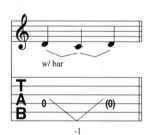

VIBRATO BAR SCOOP: Depress the bar just before striking the note, then quickly release the bar.

VIBRATO BAR DIP: Strike the note and then immediately drop a specified number of steps, then release back to the original pitch.

Additional Musical Definitions

(accent) • Accentuate note (play it louder)

(accent) • Accentuate note with great intensity

(staccato) • Play the note short

⊓ • Downstroke

∨ • Upstroke

D.S. al Coda • Go back to the sign (𝄋), then play until the measure marked "*To Coda*," then skip to the section labelled "*Coda*."

D.S. al Fine • Go back to the beginning of the song and play until the measure marked "*Fine*" (end).

Rhy. Fig. • Label used to recall a recurring accompaniment pattern (usually chordal).

Riff • Label used to recall composed, melodic lines (usually single notes) which recur.

Fill • Label used to identify a brief melodic figure which is to be inserted into the arrangement.

Rhy. Fill • A chordal version of a Fill.

tacet • Instrument is silent (drops out).

• Repeat measures between signs.

|1. |2.   • When a repeated section has different endings, play the first ending only the first time and the second ending only the second time.

NOTE: Tablature numbers in parentheses mean:
1. The note is being sustained over a system (note in standard notation is tied), or
2. The note is sustained, but a new articulation (such as a hammer-on, pull-off, slide or vibrato begins, or
3. The note is a barely audible "ghost" note (note in standard notation is also in parentheses).

guitar
SCHOOL

Guitar School takes you to class when it comes to learning how your favorite artists play. Every book comes complete with lessons on the guitar techniques and styles that make that artist special. Solos, riffs and all relevant guitar parts are discussed in the lessons, followed by exact transcriptions of these parts in both notes and tab. If you want to improve your chops, this series provides you with special exercises and lesson books by experts in the field. All books include tablature.

Beatles Guitar Techniques
Not only is this a stylistic analysis of the guitar licks and solos of the Beatles, but a deeper study of John, Paul and George's individual guitar concepts and techniques. A wonderful chronological sampling of early and later Beatles material is covered, complete with lessons and details on the Beatle who actually played the guitar parts. A must for any one wanting an inside look at the Beatles songs.
00660105......................................$19.95

Eric Clapton Solos
with lessons by Jesse Gress
This *Guitar School* book contains lessons with transcriptions of the solos to Eric Clapton's best work. It helps you understand as well as play the music. Includes 16 of his best, including: After Midnight (2 versions) • Lay Down Sally • Cocaine • Strange Brew.
00660088......................................$16.95

Best Of Def Leppard
This book takes you on a guided tour through the guitar styles of Def Leppard, showing the development of the Def Leppard sound. It includes lessons with theory and style information to help you incorporate the concepts behind these styles into your own playing. Includes licks from 12 classics, including: Bringin' On The Heartbreak • Love Bites • Pour Some Sugar On Me • Photograph • and more.
00660333......................................$16.95

Al DiMeola Solos
by Dan Towey
This exploration of DiMeola's music includes transcribed solos, lessons, and 17 songs: Adonea • The Embrace • Global Safari • Indigo • Kis My Axe • Last Tango For Astor • Morocco • One Night Last June • Ritmo De La Noche • Traces Of A Tear • and more.
00660336......................................$16.95

In Deep With Jimi Hendrix
In Deep With Jimi Hendrix brings you closer to the music and the artist than you've ever imagined. This is accomplished through breaking down and reassembling the solos, riffs, rhythm figures, harmony lines, ensemble parts, and more. All performance techniques and equipment are explored in detail. If you want to learn the techniques of Hendrix, this is the book for you.
00660335......................................$17.95

Jimi Hendrix Solos
13 songs from this legend, including: All Along The Watchtower • Castles Are Made Of Sand • Foxy Lady • Hey Joe • Little Wing • Purple Haze.
00660086..................$14.95

Eric Johnson
This book explores twelve tracks from Eric's two solo albums Tones and Ah Via Musicom. Transcription excerpts are provided with accompanying lessons on how to perform and study the playing techniques involved in each example.
00695002......................................$18.95

Judas Priest – Hell Bent For Lead Licks
Full analysis of over 50 Priest licks. Other highlights include an exclusive interview with both K.K. Downing and Glen Tipton about their unique sound and style, a complete discography and and track-by-track breakdown of their guitar solos.
00660089......................................$17.95

Kiss
Featuring The Guitar Styles of Ace Frehley & Paul Stanley
A master class teaching all of the essential licks and tricks by Kiss guitarists Ace Frehley, Paul Stanley, and more. Featuring songs like "Shout It Out Loud" and "Love Gun."
00696547......................................$17.95

Yngwie J. Malmsteen – Transcribed Solos
This book contains lessons with transcriptions in notes and tab of 14 of Yngwie Malmsteen's latest best solos. Dave Whitehill's instruction helps you understand as well as play the music.
00660090......................................$16.95

Megadeth – Guitar School
by Dale Turner
This book features transcriptions and lessons for the guitar styles of Dave Mustaine and Marty Friedman. Songs include: Symphony Of Destruction • Hangar 18 • Train Of Consequences • A Tout Le Monde • and more.
00660056......................................$19.95

Gary Moore
Here's an in-depth look at the guitar style of the modern rock master. Includes transcriptions of excerpts from many of Gary's best recordings in notes and tab, along with lessons on the techniques used.
00660332......................................$17.95

Ozzy Osbourne Guitar School
This book features the guitar styles of Randy Rhoads, Jake E. Lee, and Zakk Wylde. It explores Ozzy's music through transcriptions and lessons by Carl Culpepper. Songs include: Crazy Train • Shot In The Dark • Flying High Again • and more.
00660022......................................$16.95

Guitar School Presents Steve Vai
Learn nearly every technique in Steve Vai's incredible arsenal, including speed picking, whammy bar usage, exotic scales, tapping, harmonics, rhythms, and more! This book features instructions and tips as well as transcriptions in notes and tab of songs like "Touching Tongues," "For The Love Of God," and "The Animal."
00660025......................................$17.95

Stevie Ray Vaughan: Big Blues From Texas
by Dave Rubin
Learn the hottest licks and rhythms selected from Stevie Ray's greatest songs. This song is explained and analyzed through in-depth lessons and transcriptions. 15 songs, including: Pride And Joy • Scuttle Buttin' • Empty Arms • Love Sruck Baby • and more.
.....................................$17.95

Muddy Waters – Deep Blues And Good News
by Dave Rubin
Guitar transactions and detailed lessons of 15 great tunes, including: Honey Bee • Rollin' And Tumblin' • You Shook Me • and more. This is a unique opportunity to get inside Muddy's early country-based blues (in open and standard tunings), his hard-edged slide, and the electric lead guitar stylings of his esteemed sidemen.
00660052......................................$14.95

Prices, content, and availability subject to change without notice

FOR MORE INFORMATION, SEE YOUR LOCAL MUSIC DEALER, OR WRITE TO:

HAL•LEONARD®
CORPORATION
7777 W. BLUEMOUND RD. P.O. BOX 13819 MILWAUKEE, WI 53213

0197

RECORDED VERSIONS
The Best Note-For-Note Transcriptions Available

RECORDED VERSIONS GUITAR

ALL BOOKS INCLUDE TABLATURE

00694909 Aerosmith – Get A Grip $19.95	00660099 Jimi Hendrix – Radio One $24.95	00690055 Red Hot Chili Peppers –
00690199 Aerosmith – Nine Lives $19.95	00690280 Jimi Hendrix – South Saturn Delta $19.95	Bloodsugarsexmagik $19.95
00690146 Aerosmith – Toys in the Attic $19.95	00694919 Jimi Hendrix – Stone Free $19.95	00690090 Red Hot Chili Peppers – One Hot Minute . $22.95
00694865 Alice In Chains – Dirt $19.95	00690038 Gary Hoey – Best Of $19.95	00694892 Guitar Style Of Jerry Reed $19.95
00660225 Alice In Chains – Facelift $19.95	00660029 Buddy Holly $19.95	00694937 Jimmy Reed – Master Bluesman $19.95
00694925 Alice In Chains – Jar Of Flies/Sap $19.95	00660169 John Lee Hooker – A Blues Legend $19.95	00694899 R.E.M. – Automatic For The People $19.95
00694932 Allman Brothers Band – Volume 1 . . . . . $24.95	00690054 Hootie & The Blowfish –	00694898 R.E.M. – Out Of Time $19.95
00694933 Allman Brothers Band – Volume 2 . . . . . $24.95	Cracked Rear View $19.95	00690014 Rolling Stones – Exile On Main Street . . . $24.95
00694934 Allman Brothers Band – Volume 3 . . . . . $24.95	00690143 Hootie & The Blowfish –	00690186 Rolling Stones – Rock & Roll Circus $19.95
00694877 Chet Atkins – Guitars For All Seasons . . . $19.95	Fairweather Johnson $19.95	00690135 Otis Rush Collection $19.95
00694918 Randy Bachman Collection $22.95	00694905 Howlin' Wolf $19.95	00690133 Rusted Root – When I Woke $19.95
00694880 Beatles – Abbey Road $19.95	00690136 Indigo Girls – 1200 Curfews $22.95	00690031 Santana's Greatest Hits $19.95
00694891 Beatles – Revolver $19.95	00694938 Elmore James –	00694805 Scorpions – Crazy World $19.95
00694863 Beatles –	Master Electric Slide Guitar $19.95	00690150 Son Seals – Bad Axe Blues $17.95
Sgt. Pepper's Lonely Hearts Club Band . . $19.95	00690167 Skip James Blues Guitar Collection $16.95	00690128 Seven Mary Three – American Standards . $19.95
00690174 Beck – Mellow Gold $17.95	00694833 Billy Joel For Guitar $19.95	00690076 Sex Pistols – Never Mind The Bollocks . . . $19.95
00690175 Beck – Odelay $17.95	00694912 Eric Johnson – Ah Via Musicom $19.95	00120105 Kenny Wayne Shepherd – Ledbetter Heights $19.95
00694931 Belly – Star $19.95	00690169 Eric Johnson – Venus Isle $22.95	00690196 Silverchair – Freak Show $19.95
00694884 The Best of George Benson $19.95	00694799 Robert Johnson – At The Crossroads $19.95	00690130 Silverchair – Frogstomp $19.95
00692385 Chuck Berry $19.95	00693185 Judas Priest – Vintage Hits $19.95	00690041 Smithereens – Best Of $19.95
00692200 Black Sabbath –	00690073 B. B. King – 1950-1957 . . . . $24.95	00694885 Spin Doctors – Pocket Full Of Kryptonite . $19.95
We Sold Our Soul For Rock 'N' Roll . . . $19.95	00690098 B. B. King – 1958-1967 . . . . $24.95	00690124 Sponge – Rotting Pinata $19.95
00690115 Blind Melon – Soup $19.95	00690099 B. B. King – 1962-1971 . . . . $24.95	00690161 Sponge – Wax Ecstatic $19.95
00690241 Bloodhound Gang – One Fierce Beer Coaster . $19.95	00690134 Freddie King Collection $19.95	00120004 Steely Dan – Best Of $24.95
00690028 Blue Oyster Cult – Cult Classics $19.95	00694903 The Best Of Kiss $24.95	00694921 Steppenwolf, The Best Of $22.95
00690219 Blur $19.95	00690157 Kiss – Alive $19.95	00694957 Rod Stewart – Acoustic Live $22.95
00694935 Tracy Bonham – The Burdens Of Being Upright $17.95	00690163 Mark Knopfler/Chet Atkins – Neck and Neck $19.95	00690021 Sting – Fields Of Gold $19.95
00694935 Boston: Double Shot Of $22.95	00690202 Live – Secret Samadhi $19.95	00120081 Sublime $19.95
00690237 Meredith Brooks – Blurring the Edges . . . $19.95	00690070 Live – Throwing Copper $19.95	00690242 Suede – Coming Up $19.95
00690043 Cheap Trick – Best Of $19.95	00690018 Living Colour – Best Of $19.95	00694824 Best Of James Taylor $16.95
00690171 Chicago – Definitive Guitar Collection . . . $22.95	00694954 Lynyrd Skynyrd, New Best Of $19.95	00694887 Thin Lizzy – The Best Of Thin Lizzy $19.95
00690010 Eric Clapton – From The Cradle $19.95	00694956 Yngwie Malmsteen – Fire And Ice $19.95	00690238 Third Eye Blind $19.95
00660139 Eric Clapton – Journeyman $19.95	00690239 Bob Marley – Legend $19.95	00690022 Richard Thompson Guitar $19.95
00694869 Eric Clapton – Live Acoustic $19.95	00690239 Matchbox 20 – Yourself or Someone Like You . $19.95	00690267 311 . . . . $19.95
00694873 Eric Clapton – Timepieces $19.95	00690020 Meat Loaf – Bat Out Of Hell I & II $22.95	00690030 Toad The Wet Sprocket $19.95
00694896 John Mayall/Eric Clapton – Bluesbreakers $19.95	00690244 Megadeath – Cryptic Writings $19.95	00690228 Tonic – Lemon Parade $19.95
00694940 Counting Crows – August & Everything After $19.95	00690011 Megadeath – Youthanasia $19.95	00694411 U2 – The Joshua Tree $19.95
00690197 Counting Crows – Recovering the Satellites . $19.95	00690236 Mighty Mighty Bosstones – Let's Face It . $19.95	00690039 Steve Vai – Alien Love Secrets $24.95
00690118 Cranberries – The Best of $19.95	00690040 Steve Miller Band Greatest Hits $19.95	00690172 Steve Vai – Fire Garden $24.95
00694941 Crash Test Dummies – God Shuffled His Feet $19.95	00690225 Moist – Creature $19.95	00660137 Steve Vai – Passion & Warfare $24.95
00694840 Cream – Disraeli Gears $19.95	00694802 Gary Moore – Still Got The Blues $19.95	00690023 Jimmie Vaughan – Strange Pleasures . . . $19.95
00690007 Danzig 4 . . . . $19.95	00690103 Alanis Morissette – Jagged Little Pill . . . $19.95	00660136 Stevie Ray Vaughan – In Step $19.95
00690184 DC Talk – Jesus Freak $19.95	00694958 Mountain, Best Of $19.95	00694835 Stevie Ray Vaughan – The Sky Is Crying . . $19.95
00660186 Alex De Grassi Guitar Collection $19.95	00694895 Nirvana – Bleach $19.95	00690015 Stevie Ray Vaughan – Texas Flood $19.95
00694831 Derek And The Dominos –	00694913 Nirvana – In Utero $19.95	00694776 Vaughan Brothers – Family Style $19.95
Layla & Other Assorted Love Songs . . . $19.95	00694883 Nirvana – Nevermind $19.95	00690217 Verve Pipe, The – Villains $19.95
00690187 Dire Straits – Brothers In Arms $19.95	00690026 Nirvana – Acoustic In New York $19.95	00120026 Joe Walsh – Look What I Did... . . . . $24.95
00690191 Dire Straits – Money For Nothing $24.95	00120112 No Doubt – Tragic Kingdom $22.95	00694789 Muddy Waters – Deep Blues $24.95
00690182 Dishwalla – Pet Your Friends $19.95	00690273 Oasis – Be Here Now $19.95	00690071 Weezer $19.95
00660178 Willie Dixon – Master Blues Composer . . . $24.95	00690159 Oasis – Definitely Maybe $19.95	00690286 Weezer – Pinkerton $19.95
00690089 Foo Fighters $19.95	00690121 Oasis – (What's The Story) Morning Glory $19.95	00694970 Who, The – Definitive Collection A-E . . . $24.95
00690042 Robben Ford Blues Collection $19.95	00690204 Offspring, The – Ixnay on the Hombre . . $17.95	00694971 Who, The – Definitive Collection F-Li . . . $24.95
00694920 Free – Best Of $18.95	00690203 Offspring, The – Smash $17.95	00694972 Who, The – Definitive Collection Lo-R . . . $24.95
00690222 G3 Live – Satriani, Vai, Johnson $22.95	00694830 Ozzy Osbourne – No More Tears $19.95	00694973 Who, The – Definitive Collection S-Y . . . $24.95
00694894 Frank Gambale – The Great Explorers . . . $19.95	00694855 Pearl Jam – Ten $19.95	
00694807 Danny Gatton – 88 Elmira St $19.95	00690053 Liz Phair – Whip Smart $19.95	
00690127 Goo Goo Dolls – A Boy Named Goo $19.95	00690176 Phish – Billy Breathes $22.95	
00690117 John Gorka Collection $19.95	00690240 Phish – Hoist $19.95	
00690114 Buddy Guy Collection Vol. A-J $19.95	00693800 Pink Floyd – Early Classics $19.95	
00690193 Buddy Guy Collection Vol. L-Y $19.95	00694967 Police – Message In A Box Boxed Set . . . $70.00	
00694798 George Harrison Anthology $19.95	00690125 Presidents of the United States of America . $19.95	
00690068 Return Of The Hellecasters $19.95	00690195 Presidents of the United States of America II $22.95	
00692930 Jimi Hendrix – Are You Experienced? $19.95	00694974 Queen – A Night At The Opera $19.95	
00692931 Jimi Hendrix – Axis: Bold As Love $19.95	00694910 Rage Against The Machine $19.95	
00660192 The Jimi Hendrix – Concerts $24.95	00690145 Rage Against The Machine – Evil Empire . $19.95	
00692932 Jimi Hendrix – Electric Ladyland $24.95	00690179 Rancid – And Out Come the Wolves $22.95	
00690218 Jimi Hendrix – First Rays of the New Rising Sun $24.95		